BPB

WITHDRAWN

English Pastoral Poetry

Twayne's English Authors Series

Kinley E. Roby, Editor
Northeastern University

TEAS 348

English Pastoral Poetry

By James Sambrook
University of Southampton

Twayne Publishers • *Boston*

English Pastoral Poetry

James Sambrook

Copyright © 1983 by G. K. Hall & Company
All Rights Reserved
Published by Twayne Publishers
A Division of G. K. Hall & Company
70 Lincoln Street
Boston, Massachusetts 02111

Book Production by Marne B. Sultz

Book Design by Barbara Anderson

Printed on permanent/durable acid-free
paper and bound in the United States of
America.

Library of Congress Cataloging in Publication Data

Sambrook, James.
    English pastoral poetry.

    (Twayne's English authors series; TEAS 348)
    Bibliography: p. 150
    Includes index.
    1. Pastoral poetry, English—History and criticism.
I. Title. II. Series.
PR509.P3S35   1983   821'.009'321734   82–23222
ISBN 0–8057–6834–3

Contents

About the Author

A. J. Sambrook, born 1931, educated at Worcester College, Oxford, and the University of Nottingham, has been professor of English at the University of Southampton since 1981. His publications include *A Poet Hidden, the Life of Richard Watson Dixon, 1833–1900* (1962); editions of *The Scribleriad* and *The Difference between Verbal and Practical Virtue* for the Augustan Reprint Society (1967); James Thomson's *The Seasons* and *The Castle of Indolence*, edited with an introduction and notes (1972); William Cobbett; *An Author Guide* (1973); *Pre-Raphaelitism*, a collection of critical essays, edited with an introduction and notes (1974); an edition of Thomson's *The Seasons*, for the Oxford English Texts series (1981); and over a hundred articles and reviews in various learned journals. His edition of James Thomson's *Liberty, The Castle of Indolence, and Other Poems* (Oxford English Texts) is now in the press. He is currently writing a critical biography of James Thomson to be published by the Clarendon Press, and a study of the cultural and intellectual context of English literature, 1700–1789, to be published as a volume in the Longman's History of English Literature.

Preface

The main substance of this book is a short, descriptive history of
general tendencies and individual achievements in English nondramatic pastoral poetry from the sixteenth to the beginning of the
nineteenth century, a period which saw the establishment, varied
adaptation, and decay of the genre. The primary aim is to trace the
development of forms and conventions, rather than to discuss any
single, distinct idea, attitude, or perspective; for pastoral forms may
embrace a variety of ideas, attitudes, or perspectives. As most pastoral
conventions come from Theocritus and Virgil, this history is preceded
by an account of classical origins.

I do not define pastoral in the extended sense employed by Empson and many subsequent critics. In this study, pastoral is the kind
of poetry that takes as its subject shepherds or other rustics and generally represents them as free from the vices and sorrows of men
living in more complex societies; or it is that kind of poetry in which
poets disguised as shepherds debate their craft or other topics. In
order to accommodate my work within the present series I have
ignored, except for rare passing references, pastoral drama and prose
romance: most of the poems I treat are on the scale of, and have
forms roughly comparable with, the idylls of Theocritus and eclogues
of Virgil, or the songs inserted in those works. However, I have found
it expedient from time to time to step over those formal boundaries.
There are obvious reasons for pursuing the pastoral of Spenser, Drayton, and Wordsworth into their quasi-epical writings, and for touch-
ing upon mock-pastoral, town-eclogue, or antipastoral. My occasional
excursions into the traditions of descriptive or reflective rural verse
that stem from Horace and from Virgil's *Georgics* are perhaps less
easy to defend in general, but will, I hope, appear justifiable, each in
its context.

The central authors in the English pastoral tradition are Theocritus, Virgil, Sidney, Spenser, Milton, Pope, and Wordsworth: my

study hangs upon these, and upon such important secondary figures as Sannazaro, Drayton, Marvell, Gay, and Goldsmith; but I have not thought it necessary to give each poet a space proportionate to his greatness. Minor pastoral poetry is generously represented, as displaying the norm in those centuries when pastoral was the most admired form of minor poetry and proved irresistably attractive to minor poets. Being concerned with tradition, rather than individual talent, I have for the most part avoided biographical and bibliographical detail. I have written as simply as possible, but have assumed some general knowledge of literature, and of the social and intellectual conditions under which the literature of certain periods was written.

I am grateful to the Cambridge University Press for permission to quote from R. C. Trevelyan's translation of the *Idylls of Theocritus*, and to Dalhousie University for providing me with a research fellowship, during the tenure of which, in 1968–69, most of this book was written.

James Sambrook

University of Southampton

Chronology

Dates before 1500 are of composition; after 1500, of publication.

ca. 270 B.C.	*Idylls*, Theocritus.
ca. 100 B.C.	*Lament for Adonis*, Bion.
ca. 100 B.C.	*Lament for Bion*, attributed to Moschus.
42–37 B.C.	*Eclogues*, Virgil (70–19).
ca. 57	*Eclogues*, Calpurnius Siculus.
ca. 285	*Eclogues*, Nemesianus.
ca. 1320	*Eclogues*, Dante (1265–1321).
1346–1357	*Eclogues*, Petrarch (1304–74).
1347–1370	*Eclogues*, Boccaccio (1313–75).
1465–1498	*Eclogues*, "Mantuan," i.e., G. B. Spagnuoli (1448–1516).
ca. 1470	"Robene and Makyne," Robert Henryson (1430?–1508).
1502	*Arcadia*, Jacopo Sannazaro (1456–1530).
1515–1520	*Eclogues*, Alexander Barclay (1476–1552).
1526	*Piscatorial Eclogues*, Sannazaro.
1563	*Eglogs*, Barnabe Googe (1540–94).
1579	*Shepheardes Calender*, Edmund Spenser (1552?–99).
1589	*Eglogue Gratulatorie*, George Peele (1558?–97).
1590	*Countess of Pembroke's Arcadia*, i.e., "New Arcadia" ("Old Arcadia" written 1580), Sir Philip Sidney (1554–86). *Meliboeus*, Thomas Watson (1557?–92).
1593	*Idea, the Shepheards Garland*, Michael Drayton (1563–1631.
1594	*Affectionate Shepherd*, Richard Barnfield (1574–1627).

1595 *Astrophel, Dolefull Lay of Clorinda, Colin Clouts Come Home Againe*, Spenser.

1596 *Faerie Queene*, books 4–6, Spenser.

1600 *England's Helicon*, enlarged 1614.

1603 *Englandes Mourning Garment*, Henry Chettle (d. 1607?).

1606 *Poemes*, including "Eglogs," Drayton.

1613–1616 *Britannia's Pastorals*, books 1–2, William Browne (1590?–1645).

1614 *Shepheards Pipe*, Browne.

1615 *Shepheards Hunting*, George Wither (1588–1667).

1619 *Poems*, including "Pastorals," Drayton.

1622 *Faire-Virtue*, Wither.

1627 Poems, including "Shepheards Sirena," Drayton.

1630 *Muses Elizium*, Drayton.

1633 *Piscatorie Eclogs*, Phineas Fletcher (1582–1650).

1636 *Annalia Dubrensia.*

1638 *Poems*, Thomas Randolph (1605–35). *Obsequies to ... Edward King*, including "Lycidas."

1640 *Poems*, Thomas Carew (1594–1640).

1645 *Poems*, John Milton (1608–74).

1648 *Hesperides*, Robert Herrick (1591–1674). *Otia Sacra*, Mildmay Fane, Earl of Westmorland (d. 1665).

1649 *Lucasta*, Richard Lovelace (1618–57?).

1667 *Poems*, Katherine Philips (1631–64).

1680 *Poems*, John Wilmot, Earl of Rochester (1647–80).

1681 *Miscellaneous Poems*, Andrew Marvell (1621–78).

1689 *Poems*, Charles Cotton (1630–87).

1699 *Pills to purge Melancholy*, edited by Tom d'Urfey (1653–1723), enlarged in several editions to 1720.

1706 *Oxford and Cambridge Miscellany*, including "Pastorals," Ambrose Philips (1674–1749).

1709 Tonson's *Miscellanies*, 6, including "Pastorals," Alexander Pope (1688–1744).

1712   *Nereides or Sea Eclogues*, William Diaper (1686?–1717).

1713   *Poems*, Anne Finch, Countess of Winchilsea (1661–1720).

1714   *Shepherd's Week*, John Gay (1685–1732).

1717   *Pastorals*, Thomas Purney (1695–1728?)

1721   *Patie and Roger*, Allan Ramsay (1686–1758).

1724   *Tea-Table Miscellany*, Ramsay, enlarged 1727 and 1737.

1729   *Angling Sports ... Piscatory Eclogues*, Moses Brown (1704–87).

1730   *Poems*, Stephen Duck (1705–56).

1742   *Persian Eclogues*, William Collins (1721–59).

1748   *Collection of Poems*, edited by Robert Dodsley (1703–64), enlarged in several editions to 1782.

1766   *Poems, chiefly Pastoral*, John Cunningham (1729–73).

1767   *Partridge-Shooting*, Francis Fawkes (1720–77).

1770   *Deserted Village*, Oliver Goldsmith (1730?–74).

1783   *The Village*, George Crabbe (1754–1832).

1786   *Poems*, Robert Burns (1759–96).

1797–1799   *Poems*, Robert Southey (1774–1843).

1798   *Lyrical Ballads*, William Wordsworth (1770–1850), enlarged 1800.

1814   *Excursion* ("Ruined Cottage" written 1797), Wordsworth.

1850   *Prelude* (written 1799–1805), Wordsworth.

Chapter One

Greek

Descriptions of kindly landscapes are, doubtless, almost as old as European literature itself: there is, for instance a description in the Homeric *Hymn to Demeter* of the lovely field in which Proserpine walked. Praise of countrymen's life—explicitly or implicitly contrasting it with man's hectic and guilty existence in courts and cities—is, no doubt, almost as old as courts and cities: generations of Old Testament prophets, for instance, looked back in pious nostalgia to the innocence of the nomadic herdsmen's life before the Jews settled in Canaan and built towns. The career of King David attached a certain prestige to the occupation of the shepherd. The history of literary pastoral begins, however, in the Hellenistic or Alexandrian age of Greek literature, which followed the death of Alexander the Great in 323 B.C., and it begins in the splendid cultural metropolis of Alexandria itself.

The military conquests of Alexander, the power struggle among his generals after his death, and subsequent political settlement which established Greek dynasties in Macedonia, Persia, and Egypt, signaled the decline of the autonomous Greek city-state, and served enormously to extend Greek civilization. "The creative impulses evoked by Alexander's career forbade anything ever to be quite the same as before."[1] The whole concept of the *polis*, or city-state, gave way to that of the *oecumene*, or whole inhabited world—that is, a world inhabited by men sharing the same civilization. Poetry of the Alexandrian age is marked by a new eclecticism, which one might regard as a kind of literary ecumenism. Instead of always working strictly and exclusively within the older, classical "kinds" of epic, lyric, and dramatic poetry, Alexandrian poets combined various ancient kinds, and occasionally freshened them by bringing in features of

popular song which had never before found formal literary expression. Notwithstanding this, these poets are extremely learned;
they write with a highly self-conscious artifice, and all too frequently
strain after novelties of idiom and construction. If the number of his
followers be a measure of a man's greatness, Theocritus (fl. ca. 270
B.C.) is undoubtedly the greatest Alexandrian poet.

He was born in all probability at Syracuse in Sicily, and before he
came to Alexandria he spent part of his life in Cos, an island off
the southwest coast of Anatolia and a favorite place of abode for men
of letters. Thirty poems collected over his name—though not all are
his—are called *eidullia*, or idylls, in an ancient commentary upon his
verse. The Greek word does not occur elsewhere, but presumably is
related to *eidullon*, that is, "a little shape, or appearance." In Latin
the word *idyllium* was applied to short poems on various subjects.
The modern English word "idyll" takes its meaning, of course, from
its connection with the writings of Theocritus, particularly those on
rustic themes.

These thirty Theocritean idylls cover a wide range of different
subjects and "kinds"—extending from an eight verse epigram ("The
Honey Thief," idyll 19) to an episodic miniature epic ("Heracles the
Lion-Slayer," 25) which runs to nearly three hundred verses. Neither
of those can, as it happens, be attributed with certainty to Theocritus,
but the idylls that are accepted as firmly his include mimes with urban
settings (2, 15), *paidika*, or homosexual love-lyrics (29, 30), eulogies
of kings (16, 17), a poetical epistle accompanying the present of
a distaff to his friend's wife (28), an epithalamium for Helen and
Menelaus (18), and verses on other mythological subjects such as
the ridiculous love of Polyphemus for Galatea (11), and—in two
episodes taken from the *Argonautica* of Apollonius Rhodius—the
loss of Hylas (13), and the fight between Pollux and Amycus (22).
But the largest single group of idylls may be termed "bucolic" or
"pastoral" in the sense that they are concerned with the imagined
life of herdsmen.

The first idyll displays the eclecticism of the *Idylls* as a whole.
A long way behind this idyll lies the fact that herdsmen in the Mediterranean world did sing their own, unaffected songs. Theocritus's employ-
ment of stanzas and refrains faintly recalls a tradition of popular folk-
songs, but his meter is the dactylic hexameter—long consecrated, as
Aristotle declared, to epic and didactic poetry, and to the responses

of oracles. Theocritus writes in the Doric, that is to say a rustic dialect, but with a strong admixture of "literary" words from epic. Ritualistic utterances in the lament for Daphnis recall the Homeric hymns, and the description of the cup recalls Homer's description of epic "furnishings," such as Achilles' shield. In short, this is an elaborate, conscious, mannered art which hints at a distant origin in popular song. The highly wrought allusiveness of his work suggests that the audience for Theocritus was small and learned, and that his pastorals were not public and "popular" works as, say, classical tragedy was.

In idyll 1, a Sicilian poet-shepherd Thyrsis asks a goatherd to pipe to him; the goatherd declines, but asks Thyrsis to sing his famous song on the woes of Daphnis, and promises him, in return, a carved wooden bowl or cup, which he describes; Thyrsis sings his "bucolic song" about the sufferings and death of Daphnis, and receives gift and praise from the goatherd. The description of the cup (lines 27–56) takes up about a fifth, and the lament for Daphnis (61–142) over half of this idyll of 152 lines. So the passage of dialogue and brief indications of setting—as the two men lie at ease in the shade at noon upon a gentle knoll where the tamarisk grows—seemingly are intended merely to provide frames into which is set the song and the description of the cup.

Daphnis, a Sicilian, was the mythical founder of shepherd song; in the best attested accounts of his legend he was blinded by a nymph on account of a drunken marital infidelity, but Theocritus's highly oblique allusions are clearly to a different and obscure legend. Theocritus makes Daphnis a chaste shepherd who has angered Aphrodite, because he boasted that he could overcome sexual love, but now he is overcome by love, and is dying. He taunts Aphrodite, makes his farewell to rivers, woods, and beasts, bequeaths his pipe to Pan, and dies. The local nymphs, we are told, in a passage that was to bear infinite repetition, were not present to save Daphnis:

Where were ye then, while Daphnis pined away, where were ye, Nymphs?
Haunting Peneios' lovely valleys, or the glens of Pindos?
For not by the great river of Anapos were you dwelling,
Nor upon Etna's heights, nor yet by Akis' holy stream.[2] (66–69)

As Daphnis dies, even animals lament (71–72): "For him the jackals howled, for him the wolves: the lion even / Came forth from

the thicket to lament him when he died." After his death the ordinary
processes of nature are thrown into chaos (132–36):

> Bear violets henceforth, ye brambles, and ye thistles too,
> And upon boughs of juniper let fair narcissus bloom;
> Let all things be confounded; let the pine-tree put forth figs,
> Since Daphnis lies dying! Let the stag tear the hounds,
> And screech-owls from the hills contend in song with nightingales.

These reactions to death typify two kinds of correspondence between
man and external nature. When the natural world mourns for Daphnis, it shares the pastoral singer's grief; when it is thrown into
"unnatural" chaos, it objectifies the singer's feeling of outrage. In
both passages, which were to establish some of the most used conventions of pastoral elegy, the natural world is mysteriously linked
with human circumstances and feelings. The "pathetic fallacy," i.e.,
the imparting of human feelings and powers to objects of external
nature, appears in two of its most familiar literary forms here at
the very beginning of pastoral poetry.[3]

The lament for Daphnis takes the auditor into the world of pure
and tragic legend (139–41),

> . . . no more thread for the Fates to spin
> Was left him: down to the stream [of death] went Daphnis:
>   eddying waves closed o'er
> The man loved by the Muses, whom every Nymph held dear;

but the last seven verses of the idyll, spoken by the goatherd, lead
by natural gradations back to the commonplace setting in rustic life:

> Thyrsis, may your fair mouth for this be filled and filled again
> With honey and the honey-comb; and may you eat dried figs
> From Aigilos; for more lovely than the cricket's is your song.
> See, here's the bowl, and mark, my friend, how savourly it smells.
> In the well-spring of the Hours you might think it had been dipped.
> Come here, Kissaitha!—She is yours to milk.—Beware, you kids;
> Skip not so wantonly, or you'll have the he-goat after you.

It is a life characterized by sweetness. The idea of sweetness, so
prominent in the closing utterance of the goathead, stands out also
in the introductory dialogue (1–2, 8–9):

Thyrsis
Sweet is the whispering music of yonder pine that sings
Over the water-brooks, and sweet the melody of your pipe....

Goatherd
Sweeter, O shepherd, is your song than the melodious fall
Of yonder stream that from on high gushes down the rock....

Man and external nature share a mood of tranquillity according to yet
another form of the pathetic fallacy, by which the music of the pine
corresponds in sweetness with the shepherd's piping. The repetition
of "sweet," "sweeter" has a soothing effect, as it establishes a mood
of stability, composure, and calm delight, the mood that much later
would be called "Arcadian." Introduction and conclusion alike contrast strikingly with the lament for Daphnis: they serve to "place"
the mysterious, disturbing yet inspiring, tragedy of Daphnis' sufferings
as what it is—the material of Thyrsis' art.

In idyll 3, the next one with a pastoral setting, a goatherd gives
his flock into the care of Tityrus (1–5) and goes off to serenade
Amaryllis who lives in a cave. His song, which occupies the remaining
fifty lines of the idyll, is a rustic parody of the urban reveller's
serenade at night before the locked doors of a mistress's house. The
goatherd is a ludicrous figure, with his ugly snub nose, twitching
eyes, and aching head, but nevertheless in his persuasion to love he
links himself with all the splendid and magically successful lovers
of mythology such as Hippomanes (who won Atlanta), Adonis,
and Endymion. More characteristically he consults the omens recog-
nized by rustic superstitions (28–33, 37–39):

I found it out not long ago, when wondering if you loved me
I smeared the love-in-absence, and the petal would not stain,
But creased and withering there it lay on the soft of my arm.
A peasant, too, Paraibatis, the sieve-divining witch,
Gathering herbs the other day, told me the truth, that I
Have wholly set my heart on you, while you care naught for me....
I feel a twitch in my right eye. Can it be that portends
That I shall see her?

The mood of this piquant burlesque of unhappy love is very different
from the sweet-sad atmosphere in which idyll 1 is conceived.

Even farther removed from the mood of idyll 1 is idyll 4 which takes the form of a dialogue between two herdsmen, Corydon, who is tending the cattle of the absent Aegon, and Battus. There are no set songs in this sixty-three line long idyll, but the speeches, which are mostly of one, two, or three hexameters, are arranged in balanced alternation. The setting is, apparently, near the ancient town of Croton in what is now Calabria, or the "toe" of Italy. The dialogue passes easily through various subjects, Aegon's competing in the boxing competition at Olympia, Corydon's piping, the death of Amaryllis whom Battus once loved. It is interrupted when the herdsmen have to drive back straying cattle and Corydon extracts a thorn from Battus's foot, but is concluded with a short passage of bawdry concerning "milling" (58) or "working at" (61) a young girl near the cowshed. The simple grossness of human nature at the conclusion of idyll 4 contrasts with the ludicrous sentimentality of idyll 3 as sharply as it does with the rarified love-longing of idyll 1.

Idyll 5 (150 lines) is a dialogue between a goatherd Comatas, and a shepherd Lacon. After each has accused the other of theft, they engage in a regular singing contest (80–137) which is adjudicated by Morson in favor of Comatas. There are hints that Comatas the older man was once Lacon's lover, but that Lacon has rejected him and seduces boys himself now that he is a grown man. So a fresh variety of love appears in the idylls. Sexual references are grosser and parallels between the sexuality of humans and that of farm animals are more explicit than in idyll 4. The responsive singing contest where one man's stanza is capped by the other's, the competitive boasting, and the mutual mockery or "flyting" all carry marks of a distant folk-origin for this idyll.

Idyll 6 is another singing contest, this time between two lovers, the herdsmen Daphnis and Damoetas. Daphnis reproaches Polyphemus's indifference to the amorous advances of Galatea, while Damoetas, in reply, acts the part of Polyphemus, to explain that this indifference is assumed and is part of a lover's strategy. The songs complement one another. There is no quarrel, as in idyll 5: no victory even, for the idyll concludes (42–46):

> Damoetas, when he thus had sung, kissed Daphnis, and therewith
> Gave him a pipe, while Daphnis gave his friend a shapely flute.
> Damoetas fluted, and the herdsman Daphnis played the pipe,

And soon the calves were dancing about the tender grass.
Neither had won the victory: they were both invincible.

Peace and joy are expressed in music, and when the calves dance,
the natural world itself seems to share man's mood, and respond to his
art. The perfect equal love of the two herdsmen is contrasted implicitly with the unhappy, frustrated love of Polyphemus and Galatea,
who are fated never to be united, but always to play alternately the
parts of pursuer and pursued, whether Galatea is the wooer, as here,
or Polyphemus, as in idyll 11 (see below). The setting is beside
a stream in summer at noon, and the harmonious reposeful atmosphere is the same as the setting for idyll 1.

Idyll 7 (157 lines long) is the last of the bucolic idylls which are
indubitably by Theocritus.[4] The setting is very exactly localized on
the island of Cos.[5] The narrator is Simichidas, apparently a persona
or mask for Theocritus himself. Simichidas journeys with two friends
from the town of Cos to take part in a harvest festival at the estate
of an aristocratic family. On the way they meet a goatherd Lycidas
who is celebrated locally as a poet, and to beguile the journey Lycidas
and Simichidas sing in turn. Lycidas sings (52–89) of his own
love for Ageanax who is to voyage to Milylene, and Simichidas
replies (96–127) with a song about a love affair of his friend Aratus.
Lycidas gives him his wild olive staff as a gift from the Muses, and
the ways of the two singers separate. The gift, it seems, is a sign
that the city-poet Simichidas is admitted to the company of rural
poets. It may be that Lycidas is some well-known contemporary in
disguise: in lines 45–48 he castigates modern writers of long poems,
perhaps with Apollonius Rhodius in mind, so the entire idyll may
be a literary allegory or masquerade; but there is no decisive evidence
on this point.

Simichidas and his companions continue their journey to the
farm, and there they luxuriate in the abundance, richness, and joy
of harvest festival:

We soon were lying joyously couched upon soft deep beds
Heaped with scented rushes and vine-leaves newly stripped.
And high above our heads there swayed and quivered many a branch
Of poplar and of elm-tree, while close beside us welled
The sacred water gushing from the cavern of the Nymphs.

Amid the shadowing foliage the brown cicalas chirped
And chattered busily without pause; and far away was heard
From the dense bramble thicket the tree-frog's fluted note.
Larks and thistle-finches sang, the turtle dove was moaning;
About the running water hovered the tawny bees.
All things breathed the scent of teeming summer and ripe fruits.
Pears at our feet lay fallen, and apples at our sides
Were rolling in abundance; and the plum-trees' tender boughs
Drooped overburdened with their load of damsons to the earth;
And mouth of jars, for four years sealed with resin, were unstopped.
   Ye Nymphs of Castaly, that haunt the steep Parnassian hill,
Did ever aged Cheiron in Pholos' rocky cave
Set before Herakles a bowl with such a vintage filled?
Did ever such a draught of nectar beguile that shepherd lout
Who dwelt beside Anapos, and pelted ships with crags,
Strong Polypheme, and set his feet capering about his folds?—
Such a draught as ye Nymphs that day made stream for us beside
Harvest Demeter's altar, upon whose mound of corn
May it be mine once more to plant the great fan, while she sits
And smiles upon us, holding sheaves and poppies in each hand.

If Simichidas and Lycidas represent Theocritus and another poet, the
harvest festival may be interpreted as an allegory of poetic creation,
in which wine and water are symbols of the poet's sources of in-
spiration, and harvest fruits the rich product of the poet's abundantly
fertile creative imagination.[6] The wine, like the wine in Keats's "Ode
to a Nightingale," carries the poet into a world of myth, where he
moves among divinities not subject to time and change. This idyll
has a romantic inwardness. Its true subject is the making of poetry
rather than the imagined joys of herdsmen, and its use of "herdsman"
as a metaphor for "poet" would be profoundly significant for the
future development of pastoral.
   The greater part of idyll 11 "The Cyclops" (19–79) consists of
Polyphemus's song in which he offers a catalog of the wealth and
delights that shall be Galatea's if she accepts his love:

I know, beautiful maiden, why it is you shun me thus.
It is because from one ear to the other, right across
The whole width of my forehead, one long shaggy eyebrow runs,
With but one eye beneath; and broad is the nose above my lip.

Nevertheless, though I be such, a thousand sheep I feed,
And from these do I draw and drink milk of the very best.
And cheese neither in summer nor in autumn do I lack,
Nor in winter's depth, but always overladen are my crates.
Then I am skilled in piping as no other Cyclops here,
And of thee, my dear sweet apple, and of myself I sing
Many a time at dead of night. Moreover eleven fawns
I am rearing for you, all with brows crescent-marked, and four bear-cubs.
   Nay, come to me, and nothing, that is yours now, shall you lack.
Leave the blue breakers of the sea to gasp against the land.
More sweetly will you pass the night beside me in my cave.
There do laurels grow, and there the slender cypress trees,
There the dark ivy, there the vine with its sweet clustering grapes;
There are cool streams of water, that from her white snows drawn
Forest-girt Etna sends me hither, an ambrosial drink.
To such delights who would prefer the sea-waves for a home? (30–48)

Galatea remains obdurate, but the Cyclops' song, "the medicine of the Muses" (1–3), soothes his own sorrow: he neglects his flocks, but he "shepherded his love in music-making, and found more comfort than money could buy." Suffering gives rise to poetry, and poetry consoles the sufferer. Though the subject is mythological, idyll 11 belongs with the other bucolic idylls of Theocritus, and Polyphemus is even more grotesque a rustic lover than the goatherd of idyll 3. The idyll was much imitated in antiquity, notably by Ovid (*Metamorphoses,* bk. 13, ll. 778ff.). Polyphemus's offerings to Galatea became the basis of a regular subgenre of pastoral, the "invitation to love," of which Marlowe's is the most famous English example (see chap. 6); but in those later imitations the grotesqueness of the tempter Polyphemus generally disappears.

    With these bucolic idylls we should consider an agricultural idyll 10 (58 lines long) which is a dialogue between two reapers in the harvest field. Love-sick Bucaeus sings the praises of his mistress (24–37); then the more virile and active Milon replies with ironic praise and sings a reaping song (42–55) full of rustic maxims:

See that the cut end of your sheaf be laid to face the West
Or the North wind; for thus it is the grain will fatten best.
They that thresh corn should shun the noonday sleep. When the sun's high,
Then is the time that chaff from straw will part most easily.

But reapers should start toiling when the lark leaves his nest,
And cease work when he sleeps; but in the noonday heat should rest.

                                                              (46–51)

Here and in the prefatory dialogue Milon's language seems to be the
closest approach in all the idylls to the possible speech of actual
rustics. Milon is the most "realistic" of Theocritus's characters, and
his workaday common sense contrasts strikingly with the erotic and
absurd sentimentalism of Bucaeus.

Several idylls are set in towns and so, strictly, should not enter
a consideration of pastoral poetry, but two of these urban idylls
require comment, because they were to have a considerable influence
upon English pastoral and mock-pastoral. These are idylls 2 and 15,
both of which belong, properly, to the genre of urban realistic
"mime," the brief dramatic scene or character sketch.

Idyll 15 (149 lines), "The Syracusan Women," is set in Alexandria. Two inquisitive and silly women, Praxinoa and Gorgo, chatter
at home about their clothes, and the failings of their husbands and
servants. Then they go through the streets, jostled by the crowds to
attend Queen Arsinoe's celebration of the Festival of Adonis at the
palace. Praxinoa's volubility and broad Sicilian vowels are mocked
by a man in the crowd, but the ensuing argument is cut short when
a woman comes forward to sing a hymn to Adonis (100–144). The
comic realism of the first two-thirds of this idyll provided a fruitful
model for many eighteenth-century variations of the "Town Eclogue"
type.

Idyll 2, "The Sorceress," is a dramatic monologue by Simaetha,
who has been deserted by her lover Delphis and now seeks to recapture his love by the use of magic. After asking her slave Thestylis
to prepare materials for her spells, she utters incantations in a series
of highly wrought quatrains, with a recurrent refrain (17–63):

> Even as now I melt this wax by the aid of Hekate,
> So speedily may Myndian Delphis melt away through love.
> And even as turns this brazen wheel by Aphrodite's power,
> So restlessly may he too turn and turn around my doors.
>   O magic wheel, draw hither to my house the man I love....
> Horse-madness is a herb that grows in Arcady,[7] and maddens
> All the colts that range the hills, and the fleet-footed mares.
> Even so frenzied may I now see Delphis: to this house

May he speed like a madman from the oily wrestling school.
O magic wheel, draw hither to my house the man I love.

(28–32, 48–52)

When Thestylis has gone to complete the spells before Delphis' door, Simaetha recalls the course of her love affair (64–166, the end), punctuating her words with a refrain, "Mark, Lady Moon, whence came my love." There is a splendid and passionate abandon in the grief and sexual hunger of this love-crazed woman that sets her beside the Medea of Apollonius Rhodius; but, in keeping with his usual practice in pastoral idylls, Theocritus chooses to represent the passion of an obscure commoner, rather than of a princess. That comparison is not too farfetched which has sometimes been made between Simaetha and Martha Ray. Both Theocritus and Wordsworth "make the incidents of common life interesting by tracing in them, truly though not ostentatiously, the primary laws of our nature; chiefly, as far as regards the manner in which we associate ideas in a state of excitement."[8]

Theocritus's technique is that of the dramatist (as, indeed, Wordsworth's too often was, according to Coleridge). His invented and deliberately unheroic characters utter soliloquies or engage in dialogues, sometimes in a framework of description and reflection by the poet, but more often within a wholly objectified narrative framework. The idylls span a long scale of notes from the nobly elegiac to the grotesquely gross. Theocritus makes love and song the central motifs of pastoral poetry. Countless generations of later pastoralists borrow, often at second, third, or umpteenth hand, his devices—the literary-cum-rustic language, the song contest, the elegy, the pathetic fallacy, the folklore and the rest. Some, though they are regrettably few, recapture Theocritus's humor, which remains delicately on the edge of burlesque; but very few have his understanding of human nature.

Among the spurious or doubtful idylls attributed to Theocritus it is possible to see the growth of a tradition of pastoral writing. Idyll 8 is a competent imitation while idyll 9 is a bad imitation of the authentic idylls 5 and 6. Both are catalogs of the delights of country life, though 9, with its "acorns roasting on the fire and puddings in the pots," is more earthy than 8. Idyll 21 asserts that poverty alone teaches men to develop handicrafts and supports this proposition with the story of two poor fishermen: the poem is thus the distant ancestor of the "piscatory eclogue." Idyll 27 in which the shepherd Daphnis courts a shepherdess and draws her into a wood where, after a token show of resistance, she yields to him, has been attributed variously to Theocritus, to Bion, and to Moschus, but fairly certainly is not by Theocritus. The writer provides enough salacious circumstantial detail of the seduction scene to encourage later writers to provide more. The idyll was imitated several times in seventeenth-century England: Dryden's is probably the most indecent of the regular "literary" versions.

A tradition of pastoral elegy begun in Theocritus's idyll 1 is continued by Bion of Smyrna in Anatolia, and by the unknown author of the *Lament for Bion*, which was long attributed to Moschus of Syracuse. Bion's *Lament for Adonis* describes the scene as the corpse of Adonis, killed by the boar he was hunting, is laid upon Aphrodite's bed. The poem has a wild and heated eroticism which doubtless reflects the character of the cult of Adonis in Bion's native Anatolia. The Adonis myth allegorized the death of the old year and birth of the new, so with the return of spring Adonis would come and again be united with Aphrodite, and the generative life of Nature would begin once more. The last verses of the Lament for Adonis read: "Cease thy laments today, Cytherea; stay thy dirges. / Again must thou lament, again must thou weep another year."[9] This glance into the future, not without a hint of hope, was to be a continuing feature of the pastoral elegy. The mountain nymphs and Adonis' hounds join Aphrodite in mourning, and so do the hills, the forests, the rivers, and the springs. Here again is the pathetic fallacy, which in this case is clearly no more or less than a literary counterpart to the primitive religious belief that underlay the Adonis myth.[10] Originally it was the death of vegetation as the old year died that was being mourned, but now withering vegetation itself becomes the mourner.

The *Lament for Bion* is clearly modeled upon the lament for Daphnis in Theocritus's idyll 1. All nature is called upon to weep for the dead Bion: Apollo, Pan, the satyrs, the priapoi, Galatea, and other nymphs all join the mourners, and every famous city where any great poet had lived shares the general lamentation. Lines 99–104 utter what was to become one of the great poignant commonplaces of pastoral elegy: "Alas, when in the garden wither the mallows, the green celery, and the luxuriant curled anise, they live again thereafter and spring up another year, but we men, we that are tall and strong, we that are wise, when once we die, unhearing sleep in the hollow earth, a long sleep without end or wakening."[11]

The subject of this lament is not a mythological Daphnis or Adonis, but the historical Bion. Bion is described as a "neatherd," and as a singer who bequeaths his gift of song to the author of this lament (93–97), much as Lycidas makes over his staff, the gift of the Muses, to Simichidas. More obviously than in Theocritus, "herdsmen" has become a metaphor for "poet," and the "bucolic masquerade" emerges very much more clearly as a distinctive element in pastoral poetry.

The Greeks bequeath to later pastoralists a form consisting of a song, or songs, within a tenuously dramatic frame, and an eclectic principle of style which can best be described as artificial rusticity. They provide furnishings and phrases that would bear continual reuse in a great variety of contexts, and they sketch a sweet pastoral landscape which will flower into Arcadia under the hands of later poets. Their main subjects are the power of love and the consolation of art, but they throw out undeveloped hints of correspondences between external nature and the feelings of men. Though they do not overtly allegorize, they open up for later poets the possibilities of using Arcadia, and its innocent resident shepherds, as a moral and aesthetic norm, while the shepherd heroes of Theocritus, ranging from Daphnis to Lycidas to Polyphemus, proved infinitely suggestive as figures of power or pathos. The most fruitful features of Theocritean pastoral developed into a convention quite early—as early as Virgil—but perhaps only Virgil himself, and Spenser among his successors, matched the versatility of Theocritus.

Chapter Two

Classical Latin

The writings of Bion and Moschus were joined to the idylls of Theocritus in a collection of bucolic verse made by Artemidorus in the time of Sulla (138–78 B.C.). By then Theocritus and his Greek followers in pastoral poetry were classics, but their influence upon the European pastoral tradition was to be less direct than that of Virgil (70–19 B.C.).

Virgil was the son of a farmer living in the region of Mantua in Cisalpine Gaul, which Gallic origin inclines some critics to see a Celtic, "romantic" spirit in Virgil's writings. After a period of study in Cremona, Milan, and Rome, Virgil returned to his Mantuan farm where about 43 B.C., at the age of twenty-seven, he began the composition of a series of bucolic poems imitating and emulating Theocritus. Virgil may have lost his farm for a while in the confiscations of 41 B.C. (see below). His bucolic poems were published probably in 37 B.C., and earned immediate and lasting applause. It is not known what collective title he gave them, but the early editors called them *Eclogae*—"Eclogues," or selected poems. The ten poems as Virgil artfully and symmetrically arranged them in the published collection are certainly not in chronological order of composition. What this order was no one knows, but it will be convenient here to deal with the eclogues in groups, taking what are, broadly speaking, the most Theocritean ones first.

Eclogue 2 tells of the Shepherd Corydon who burns with unrequited love for the beautiful Alexis: "Formosum pastor Corydon ardebat Alexin" (line 1). The first two words, expressing as they do the shepherd's desire for the beautiful, distill the essential subject matter of pastoral poetry. Most of the eclogue (lines 6–68, the end) consists of unhappy Corydon's love-song or rather a few portions of his song, because we are told that the recital of it continued from noon to sunset. The setting is an ideal Sicilian landscape which is evidently based upon hints in various idylls of Theocritus (3, 5, 11), but has a sensuousness, even lushness, that Theocritus rarely attains:

> See!
> The Nymphs bring basket-loads of lilies for you.
> The shining Naiad plucks pale violets and poppy-heads,
> Unites them with narcissus and sweet-smelling fennel.
> Entwines them with cassia and other fragrant herbs,
> And spangles the dark hyacinth with gaudy marigold.
> I will gather you quinces of delicate silvery bloom,
> Chestnuts that Amaryllis loved when she was mine,
> And waxy, yellow plums. (45–53)

Like the goatherd in Theocritus's idyll 3, Corydon compares himself to the great lovers of mythology, and like Damoetas in idyll 6 he plays the part of Polyphemus; but by far the greatest number of Theocritean echoes in this very derivative eclogue come from idyll 11, where the Sicilian monster Polyphemus, a prototype of the Passionate Shepherd in so many later pastorals, proclaims his love for the obdurate Galatea, offers her all his wealth and devotion, and finally condemns himself, as Corydon does here, for wasting time upon so fickle an object for his love. In a sense, Virgil out-Greeks the Greek in putting the phrases of the heterosexual lover of idyll 11 into the mouth of a homosexual Corydon. This alteration adds an extra twist of incongruity to what is, in any case, a gently ironic work; for, like Theocritus in idyll 3 but less obviously, Virgil is mocking the desperate earnestness and pretensions of this rustic lover.

Eclogue 3 is a singing match arising out of a quarrel (like Theocritus's idyll 5); one of the prizes is a pair of carved cups (cf. the one cup in idyll 1); and the result is a tie (cf. idyll 6). There are contemporary references when one of the singers, Menalcas, praises the poet-statesman Pollio, a patron of Virgil (84–89), and abuses Maevius and Bavius the poetasters (90, 91). As in Eclogue 2, Virgil handles his shepherd-lovers with a very light, half-humorous touch, but the setting evokes the finest poetry.

In Eclogue 5, another dialogue, Virgil again unites motifs from various Theocritean idylls, adds a touch of contemporary relevance with references to the deification of Julius Caesar, and imbues the

whole with his characteristic feeling for external nature. The setting
for two neatly paralleled songs which make up the greater part of
this eclogue is a cave, the mouth of which is hung with clusters of
wild grapes: that is, a holy place dedicated to worship and poetry.
Here Mopsus mourns (20–44) the death of Daphnis, i.e., the legendary founder of Sicilian pastoral song referred to in Theocritus's
idyll 1, and Menalcas celebrates his resurrection and translation to
Heaven (56–80). When Daphnis dies there is a general blight of
nature:

> Now, in furrows where we cast fat grains of barley,
> The wretched darnel and barren wild-oat spring up.
> Gone is the gentle violet, the gay narcissus gone;
> Thistles and prickly thorns rise up instead   (36–39)

When he rises to Heaven all nature rejoices:

Because of this the woods and all the countryside
And Pan, the shepherds, Dryads—all are pierced with keen delight....
For joy the shaggy mountains raise a clamour to the stars;
The very rocks, the copses now resound in song.
"He is a God" they cry, Menalcas, "He is a God."   (58–59, 62–64)

In this combination of lament for a death and hymn of rejoicing for
a resurrection Virgil attaches the ritual of the Adonis cult more firmly
to the legend of the shepherd-singer Daphnis. The apotheosis is in-
vested with a quite un-Theocritean religious fervor, which, suitably
Christianized, would become the characteristic mood of conventional
Renaissance pastoral elegy. Finally, Virgil links this work to eclogues
2 and 3 by representing Menalcas as the singer of those two, which
he identifies by their first verses:

> I will forestall you by giving you this graceful reed—
> The very pipe to which I owe my song, "The Shepherd Corydon
> Burned for the beautiful Alexis"; the same that taught me
> "Are these Meliboeus' Sheep?"   (85–87)

The identification of shepherd with poet is asserted firmly, where in
the seventh idyll of Theocritus it is merely implied: such identifications
would become normal in Renaissance pastoral.

Eclogue 7 is another singing match, in this case modeled upon the pseudo-Theocritean idyll 8. The setting is avowedly the countryside of Virgil's native Mantua, "Here Mincius lines his green shores with swaying rushes / And swarming bees drone from the sacred oak" (12–13), but Corydon and Thyrsis, the shepherds who contend in song, are "Arcadians both." In their songs they elaborate a lover's hyperbole that all things flourish at the approach and wither at the departure of the beloved, a conceit that was to echo through Renaissance and later literature.

All four eclogues mentioned above were probably written early: eclogue 8 is one of the last three that Virgil wrote but it belongs with the "Theocritean" ones. Like Theocritus's idyll 6, this is an alternation of songs rather than a regular contest. Damon sings of his unrequited love for Nysa, who is to marry a rival suitor that day, and recalls his first meeting with her:

You were a child, Nysa, when, in our orchards, I first saw you;
You and your mother gathering apples wet with dew.
I was your helper, just tall enough to reach the laden branches,
Though not yet twelve. At the first look I perished;
At the first look my soul was lost to me. (37–41)

This, like much of Damon's song, is suggested by Theocritus's idyll 11, evidently Virgil's favorite; but, unlike Polyphemus, Damon finds no consolation in song and no creative delight in an imaginative vision of nature's richness: instead, he imagines a natural world totally awry, where the wolf flies from the sheep, oaks bear apples, and alders carry narcissus blooms, echoing Theocritus's idyll 1 (132–36).

The song of the other shepherd, Alphesiboeus, is modeled upon idyll 2, but in this case the setting is rural, not urban, and a happy ending is supplied when the woman's magic spells succeed in drawing her man home to her. The two songs which make up eclogue 8 contrast different responses by two jilted lovers: the plaintive and despondent man loses his mistress, while the jealous and resolute woman gains her lover. This contrast in the fortunes of love is emphasized by a close structural correspondence, stanza by stanza, between the two songs. In the opening verses of the eclogue Virgil, apparently writing *in propria persona*, dedicates the entire work to a powerful soldier-poet (possibly Pollio, see below, eclogue 4).

At the beginning and in some phrases near the end of eclogue 10
Virgil makes his farewell to bucolic poetry:

> One last labour I pray you to favour me in, Arethusa. . . .
> Muses divine, may these verses satisfy you,
> That your poet has sung.   (1, 70, 72)

This eclogue introduces a lovesick shepherd who is no fictional figure,
but Virgil's friend Gallus, a gallant soldier and distinguished elegiac
poet who has been deserted by his mistress. He is depicted as surrounded by Arcadian shepherds and local deities who listen to the
plaintive love-song of a second Daphnis upon the point of dying for
love:

> Where were you, young Naiads, haunting what woods or glades,
> When Gallus pined for hopeless love?
> You were not detained on Parnassus or the slopes of Pindus,
> Or by the sacred spring—Aonian Aganippe.
> Even the laurels, even the tamarisks wept for him,
> Where, beneath a rock, he lay alone; pine-crowned Maenalus
> Wept for him, and so did the rocks of cold Lycaeus.   (9–15)

Parallels with the first idyll of Theocritus are evident, but Gallus is
an historical figure, a soldier and sophisticated city-poet, and his setting
is historical Arcadia, a barren, mountainous region, while his mistress,
who has left him for another soldier, journeys in the equally real,
desolate regions of Alpine snows and frozen Rhine. There is a touch
of comedy as Gallus self-indulgently throws himself into the role of
a second Daphnis and at the same time considers the possibility of
becoming a pastoral poet, but the rightful place of Gallus is in the
real world of politics and war. Pastoral retirement, in life or art, can
be no more than a diversion. Virgil thus closes his collection of
eclogues with a placing and rejection of pastoral idealism. He looks
forward to writing on higher themes and bids farewell to retirement
("shade"), doing so in a perfectly judged, simple pastoral image, as
the goatherd gets to his feet to drive his flock home:

"Surgamus: solet esse gravis cantantibus umbra" ("Let us arise:
shade is bad for singers," 75).

The remaining four eclogues owe hardly anything to Theocritus,
and their subject is not love. Although eclogue 9 has some formal

similarities to Theocritus's idyll 7, its subject matter is very different. Two countrymen meet on the road and fall into conversation, and subsequently into song. One of them, Moeris, is one of the many Mantuan farmers evicted to make way for the Triumvirate's demobilized soldiers, who had been induced to fight the Philippi campaign (42 B.C.) by the promise of a settlement of land which was to be confiscated not from their enemies, but from peaceable Italian peasants. Moeris' companion, Lycidas, speaks of the efforts of Menalcas, another farmer, to save their district from this violent and unjust expropriation:

> Yet surely I had heard that all the land was saved, from where
> The hills falls back to leave the gently-sloping spur,
> As far as the water and the old beech-trees with shattered crowns,
> All this had been saved by Menalcas and his poetry. (7–10)

Menalcas has submitted a verse-petition, but it has failed. The two rustics then while away their journey toward Mantua by praising and reciting snatches from the songs of Menalcas, who, in view of eclogue 5 (85–87), probably represents Virgil himself. The description of Menalcas's home district, quoted above, suggests a real place, the scene of the dialogue is exactly localized on the road to Mantua, and the interlocutors are found in a real and catastrophic historical situation. Such realism emphasizes contrasts between this eclogue and the superficially similar seventh idyll of Theocritus.[1] For instance, whereas Simichidas and Lycidas meet at the magical hour of noon as Simichidas walks out from the city to join a rich harvest festival—the implication being that pastoral is a delightful and relaxing diversion from involvement in city life—Virgil's Moeris and Lycidas journey in gathering darkness, under an impending storm, out of the threatened countryside toward an unknown city.

Evictions around Mantua are the subject of eclogue 1 also. Here Meliboeus's farm has been expropriated and he is taking himself, and all that he has been able to save from the disaster, away from Mantua to find a home somewhere, possibly among Scythians or Britons at the ends of the earth. On the way he encounters Tityrus who is lying at ease watching his flocks at pasture. Tityrus explains that he has been allowed to keep his farm because he went to Rome and appealed to a young, godlike man. This godlike man has been generally thought

to represent Octavian, the very person who ordered the evictions:
thus the same politico-military power that destroys the world of
Meliboeus safeguards that of Tityrus, though the two herdsmen seem
quite unaware of this paradox. Tityrus is so preoccupied with his own
good fortune that he spares no sympathy for Meliboeus beyond the
offer of supper and a night's lodging before he continues his journey
into exile. Meliboeus sadly contrasts his own unhappy fate—the terrible result of civil war—as he congratulates Tityrus on his good
fortune in escaping dispossession:

> Happy old man! Here, beside familiar streams
> And holy springs, you will seek the cool shade.
> Here the hedge has always marked your neighbor's boundary,
> Where bees of Hybla, sipping its willow-blossom and humming,
> Will often lull you gently to sleep. Over there
> Woodmen will sing to the breezes at the rock's foot;
> And turtle-doves and hoarse woodpigeons, your delight,
> Will never cease to murmur in the elm tree-tops.   (51–58)

Thus, as in eclogue 9, the beautiful, idealized north Italian landscape
is regarded with the melancholy nostalgia of an exile. The imagined,
self-sufficient, secluded world of pastoral leisure, freedom, love, and
art is fragile. Virgil acknowledges the wide gap between ideal and
real, between the desires of the poet's imagination and the actual
harsh world in which men must live. Beside the sufferings of Meliboeus, the pipings of Tityrus appear sentimental and escapist.

Tityrus appears again as the singer of eclogue 6, and he dedicates
his poem to Varus, who was mentioned in eclogue 9, and was, presumably, an actual friend or patron of Virgil; but by contrast with
9 and 1, the material of eclogue 6 is pure fantasy. Two boys and a
Naiad capture the sleeping Silenus and compel him to sing in order
to earn his release. Silenus's songs tell of the Creation, according to
the notions of the Epicurean philosopher Lucretius, and allude to the
most ancient myths—Deucalion's Flood, the age of Saturn, the punish-
ment of Prometheus, Pasiphae's unnatural sexual appetite, and many
other legends, mostly concerned with unhappiness in love. He sings
of the metamorphoses of Scylla, Tereus, and Philomela, and all the
songs that Apollo composed and taught to the laurels fringing the
river Eurotas. In thus reciting all the songs of Apollo, Silenus as-

serts that poetry takes all things as its province, fact and fiction, from the origin of the universe to the movements of the human heart. The pastoral setting of this eclogue is scarcely more than perfunctory; for the poem is a statement about poetry, not about the rural life, actual or ideal. One of Silenus's songs praises Gallus, who is the subject of eclogue 10, and the entire work, as composed by Tityrus (Virgil), is dedicated to Varus. Thus this eclogue, like others, serves to compliment Virgil's contemporaries. All the eclogues but two (2 and 7) contain some reference, open or veiled, to Virgil himself, or to his friends and patrons, for Virgil is exploring the possibility of using pastoral as literary allegory, "bucolic masquerade"—a possibility first indicated in the seventh idyll of Theocritus, and to be exploited to exhaustion in Renaissance pastoral.

Eclogue 4 is another complimentary poem. It is dedicated to the poet, soldier and statesman, Pollio, who was consul in 40 B.C. and played a leading part in the reconciliation of Octavian and Antony at Brundisium in that year, which forms the background to Virgil's prophecy of an age of peace. Virgil, again writing *in propria persona*, declares that he will sing of loftier matters:

> Muses of Theocritus, we shall attempt a grander theme.
> Coppices and humble tamarisks are not for everyone;
> If we sing of forests, let them be worthy of a Consul.
>   Ours is the last age, foretold in Sibylline verses;
> Born of Time, a new cycle of ages begins,
> Justice returns, the Golden Age begins anew,
> Its first-born comes down from Heaven above. (1–7)

The return of the Age of Saturn, the Golden Age, will coincide with the growth to manhood of a wonder-child—possibly Pollio's, or possibly the hoped-for offspring of Octavian or of Antony, both of whom had married in the year that the poem was written.[2] Christian readers, including the Emperor Constantine, St. Augustine, and Dante, identified the wonder-child with Christ; there were prayers at Rheims Cathedral in the Middle Ages for Virgil as "Prophet of the Gentiles," and even in the twentieth century commentators have made much of what appear to be echoes in eclogue 4 of the Messianic prophecies of Isaiah.[3]

Be that as it may. One thing is clear: Virgil's prophecy combines the familiar Graeco-Roman notion of cyclical world-ages with the no less common Graeco-Roman tradition of a former Golden Age. The Greek tradition, which goes back at least as far as Hesiod (possibly eighth century B.C.), was that there had been five ages of man. In the first, the Golden Age, Chronos, or Saturn in the Roman mythological system, reigned upon earth. Men lived together in perfect amity, without toil, dishonesty, sickness, or old age, and the earth, without cultivation, yielded its fruits in abundance. Then Zeus usurped the throne of Chronos, Olympians supplanted Titans, and the earth entered its Silver Age, when material conditions became harder and alternation of summer and winter became known for the first time. The decline continued through the Brazen Age, was briefly halted in the Heroic Age, but became more marked with the latest, the Iron Age, in which, to their sorrow, contemporaries of Hesoid and Virgil live. Iron Age man is sinful, and his life is full of pain, misery, and toil. Justice has long since departed for the Heavens and become the constellation Virgo. Only evil, woe, hatred, and violence remain on earth. All earlier writers placed the Golden Age in the remote past, but Virgil anticipates a revolution of the world-ages that will bring back the Golden Age in the near future. Pope was to describe pastoral poetry as "an image of the Golden Age." Virgil's two eclogues on the Mantuan expropriations are anything but that, but in eclogue 4 he firmly unites the Golden Age notion with the tradition of bucolic verse in a manner which greatly enlarges the imaginative range of pastoral.[4]

The dream of the Golden Age is, of course, one of Virgil's reactions to the historical events alluded to in eclogues 1 and 9; and the very presence of these two among the carefully interrelated poems which make up the whole tightly unified collection of eclogues[5] suggests that Virgil intends the reader to see eclogue 4 as a dream impossible to realize in the actual world. It is important to remember that all the eclogues were written during that long period of almost incessant civil war that extended from Julius Caesar's crossing of the Rubicon in 49 B.C. to Octavian's victory at Actium in 31 B.C. In the bucolic idylls of Theocritus there are no irruptions from the harsh world of politics and war, and the poet appears deliberately to be unconcerned with public issues of any kind. Love and poetry are his themes. These are Virgil's themes too, but in his pastorals they are related to the painful complexities of social life. The lighter, no more than half-serious, amatory complaints in eclogues 2 and 8, the delicate bittersweet love-melancholy of eclogue 10 and the singing contests are not mere "escape" into fantasy. They are rather an attempt on the part of their author to attain internal harmony and emotional balance in the face of external anarchy and the almost insupportable harshness of life.

Of the first eclogue Brooks Otis writes, "Pastoral, that most unhistorical of genres, has been Romanized and brought into history."[6] The real world of time and place is far more clearly evident in Virgil than in Theocritus. Admittedly, there is little geographical consistency in the *Eclogues*, partly because various landscapes function not only as settings but as symbols of states of mind and feeling:[7] features of Mantua and Sicily are blended, and, in eclogues 4, 7, 8 and 10, there are references to that mountainous region in the center of the Peloponnese called Arcadia where the worship of Pan originated—references which would provide a name for the ideal landscape of innumerable later pastoral poets.[8] Nevertheless, the deep love—the religious feeling—for the beauty and fertility of Italy that is proclaimed so majestically in the *Georgics* and the *Aeneid* informs the *Eclogues*.

Though the georgic is a literary kind quite distinct from the pastoral eclogue, it will not be out of place to refer here to the passage from the second book of Virgil's *Georgics* beginning with line 458, "O fortunatos nimium, sua si bona norint / Agricolas," which was to become the most evocative and influential panegyric of rural life in western literature:

> O happy farmers, if only they knew their luck,
> For whom, far from the clash of armaments,
> Rewarding earth unbidden pours out all they need....
> Calm security and a life without fraud,
> Rich in its own rewards, are here: the ease of broad farmlands....
> (458–60, 467–68)

The key word is "otium"[9] (translated here as "ease," but also translatable as "freedom"): it conveys the holiday feeling that we find also in that rich evocation of the harvest festival in Theocritus's idyll 7. For Virgil the aura of the Golden Age still hangs about the Italian small farmer's life, particularly when it is contrasted with the lives of citizens, courtiers, and soldiers. The picture of the hardy, virtuous, thrifty "happy husbandman" in the *Georgics* idealizes the life of the farmer hardly less than the *Eclogues* idealize the life of the herdsman, and the notion that pastoral leisure and rustic labor are complementary to one another runs through both works. Most of the herdsmen in the *Eclogues* are cultivators as well: for example, Tityrus in eclogue 1 possesses a well-balanced mixed farm, while the landscape of eclogue 2 is a farm where harvest-workers rest briefly from their toil at noon and a plowman returns home after work at evening. The *Eclogues*, like the *Georgics*, represent a glorified image of external nature made productive by the labors of man, at the same time as they show nature as the mirror of man's emotions and imaginative desires.

However, Virgil was the son of a farmer, and quite capable of writing about farming without such glorification. The one work in the *Appendix Virgilianae*, a collection of poems never published by Virgil, that can most probably be attributed to him displays a quite uncompromising realism in its treatment of rural life and labor. This is the *Moretum*, which describes the poor peasant getting up in the morning in his wretched hovel and preparing the dish of herbs and cheese which gives its name to the poem. The work is a perfect little genre painting, without sentimentality, but informed throughout with a clear-eyed, sympathetic understanding of what it is to live just above subsistence level.

In the *Eclogues* Virgil extends the range of pastoral poetry beyond the subjects treated by Theocritus, most obviously in eclogues 4, 6, 1, and 9. Love is no longer omnipresent as it was in Theocritus's bucolic idylls. It is the major theme, but the fervors of love as we find them in Theocritus are softened and quietened in Virgil: the calmness and repose of external nature serve as a counterbalance to the waywardness of human passion. On the other hand, the iron world of politics and war and suffering impinges upon the golden world of pastoral ease and freedom. Virgil allegorizes more than Theocritus, and makes much more of the correspondence between shepherd and poet. A less obvious difference between the two poets lies in their treatment of external nature. The subject of Theocritus's bucolic idylls is human love in its many aspects, and herdsmen provide the Alexandrian poet, as they were later to supply Wordsworth, with simple vehicles in whom the elemental passions may most clearly be observed. The rural setting is, of course, essential in order to define the characteristics of these simple herdsmen, but it rarely does more. Idyll 7 is the only exception, when, in the concluding verses, Theocritus conveys man's sense of nature's richness and of his own satisfied involvement in the natural scene. Virgil, who is tremulously sensitive to the beauties of external nature, constantly conveys this sense of human fulfillment within a landscape. As C. Day Lewis writes: "nature, man and deity are interfused, responding to one another immediately and without self-consciousness. They [the eclogues] are sincere, because Virgil had a deep feeling for this golden-age spirit and spontaneity, which for him still haunted the countryside."[10]

Two contemporaries and admirers of Virgil, Horace (65 B.C.– 8 B.C.) and Tibullus (died 19 B.C.), did not write idylls and eclogues but their praise of country life, particularly Horace's, was to have its part in shaping the English pastoral tradition. The amazing lyrical versatility of Horace's *Odes* was a challenge to innumerable English poets, and Horace is probably the most quoted, most imitated, and most widely influential ancient poet in English literature. His small country villa, the "Sabine Farm," was to become the prime literary symbol of a rural refuge from the cares and confusions of city life. Countless generations of English gentlemen accepted it as a practicable cultural model, and believed that Horace had taught there the art of life just as surely as elsewhere he had taught the art of poetry.

Among the *Epistles* and *Odes* are a dozen or so invitations to Horace's city friends to come and visit him at the Sabine Farm. Epistles 10, 14, and 16 contrast country life with the city. So does the sixth satire of the second book ("Hoc erat in votis") which opens,

This was one of my prayers: a little space of land with a garden, near the house a spring of living water, and a small wood besides. Heaven has fulfilled it, better and richer than my hopes. It is good. I ask no more now, Mercury, but this: make it for ever my own;[11]

and concludes with the fable of the town mouse and country mouse. The most frequently quoted Horatian statement of the joys and virtues of rural life is in the early epode 2 ("Beatus ille"):

> Happy is he who, far away from business cares,
> Like that first ancient race of men
> With his own oxen works the field his fathers tilled.[12]

Post-Renaissance imitations of these verses are countless, but, significantly, English imitators usually omitted Horace's ironic postscript where the reader learns that the speaker of this rhapsody is not the poet, but is Alfius the usurer who will, after his sentimental reverie, return to moneylending in the city. What for Horace had been satire upon the inconsistencies of human nature and the ease with which the mind can nourish mutually incompatible desires, became in most of his English imitators a simple representation of near-Arcadian bliss to be found in the contemporary countryside.

The *Elegies* of Tibullus are largely given over to tormented sexual love, but in them the countryside is equated with spiritual health, and each of the two books published in his lifetime opens with a poem in praise of country life.

The Virgilian pastoral eclogue tradition survived tenuously into the Roman Silver Age in the work of Calpurnius Siculus—the epithet "Siculus" may mean either that he came from Sicily or that he was a devotee of the Sicilian pastoral of Theocritus. He was the author of seven eclogues, written probably ca. 54–57 A.D. in the early reign of Nero. These poems closely and confessedly echo situations, ideas, and turns of expression in Virgil's eclogues. Calpurnius's eclogue 5 has a hint of the *Georgics* in that it contains precepts for the practical management of sheep and goats, but the first, fourth, and seventh eclogues are court allegories praising the new young emperor. Eclogue 1, for instance, rehandles the material of Virgil's fourth (Messianic) eclogue:

Rejoice above all, ye denizens of the woods; rejoice, ye peoples who are mine! all the herd may stray and yet no care trouble its guardian: the shepherd may neglect to close the pens at night with wattles of ash-wood—yet no robber shall bring his crafty plot upon the fold, or loosing the halters drive the bullocks off. Amid untroubled peace, the Golden Age springs to a second birth.[13]   (36–42)

In Nemesianus, the third-century Carthaginian whose *Eclogues* closely imitate those of Calpurnius, the allegorizing tendency of Latin pastoral is continued.

Chapter Three

Earlier Renaissance

Pastoral poetry was not an important literary kind in the ancient world: it was, seemingly, unknown to the classical Greeks; and though Theocritus and Virgil laid down the guidelines of a genre their Greek and Roman imitators were very few. Horace does not mention pastoral in his *Ars Poetica*; but in the Renaissance there was much criticism, and critics, rightly or wrongly building upon a foundation supplied by the late fourth- or early fifth-century commentator Servius, favored a highly allegorical interpretation of Virgil's writings. Thus when the pastoral eclogue was resuscitated as part of the general revival of classical learning in the Italian fourteenth century, it was used largely as an allegorical vehicle.

In the last two years of his life Dante (1265–1321) wrote epistolary eclogues in Latin hexameters, but the most significant of the early Italian Renaissance pastoralists is Petrarch (1304–74) who, while he was enjoying his solitary retirement at Vaucluse in 1346, began a series of Latin pastorals, the *Bucolicum Carmen*. His subjects, however, are not the joys of retirement. In his second eclogue, for instance, he mourns his patron Robert of Naples and deplores the political turmoil that followed Robert's death. The sixth and seventh eclogues—the best known—are virulent satires against the divided church and the "Babylonian captivity" of the Avignon popes. Eclogue 11, by contrast, is a moral allegory: two mourning sisters, Niobe (uncontrolled sorrow) and Fusca (reason confused with passion), on their way to the tomb of Galatea (i.e., Petrarch's dead mistress Laura) meet a third, Fulgida, who offers the consolation of reason combined with faith.

Allegory—political, autobiographical, or ecclesiastical—is the essence of Petrarch's pastorals and his eclogues can be understood only with the help of the keys provided by himself or by his friends. Petrarch wrote in a letter to one of his friends that the nature of pastoral poetry is such that it is entirely incomprehensible ("ut ... omnino non possit intellegi"), unless the author expounds it himself; and W. L. Grant, in his valuable study of the whole field of neo-Latin pastoral, sums up the situation well: "in Petrarch's work the eclogue has become a vehicle for the most medieval kind of riddling; *the allusions are everything, and the classical form is wholly incidental to the mystification.*"[1]

The first six of the sixteen *Buccolicum Carmen* by Boccaccio (1313–75) were probably written before 1350, when he first saw Petrarch's work in this kind; but the remainder confess the influence of the older poet, whom Boccaccio hailed as his master in the art of pastoral. Most of Boccaccio's eclogues are political, but the most interesting are devotional. Eclogue 11, "Pantheon," contains, at 136–228, an account of Christ's birth, life, ministry, death, resurrection, and second coming, in which Christ on every appearance but one is given a different mythological name: Codrus, Lycurgus, Asclepius, Pales, Actaeon, Hercules, Hippoltyus, Phoebus and King Arthur. Grant observes: "The intention of this seems to be to insist that Christ is the sum and more than the sum of all the virtues belonging to the heroes of antiquity."[2] Boccaccio's allegory is nothing if not ingenious. For instance, when King Arthur dispatches his Knights of the Round Table upon their quests, he is Christ sending out his Apostles, and when Hercules recovers the cattle from Cacus, he is Christ harrowing Hell and redeeming souls. Later pastoralists are less promiscuously eclectic, and when they seek to identify Christ or God with a figure from pagan mythology, they generally choose Phoebus or Pan.[3]

In the course of eclogue 14, "Olympia," the finest and most famous of the series, Boccaccio again allegorizes the life of Christ under the character of Codrus, legendary King of Athens; he also introduces the Virgin Mary as Parthenos, "the virgin," Satan as Plutarchus, and God as Archesilaus, "the Almighty." Olympia is the poet's own dead daughter who appears to him in a vision, much after the fashion of the contemporary Middle English *Pearl*, and tells him of the joys of Heaven and instructs him in the ways that he might earn a place there: "Feed your brother's hunger, give milk to the weary, help the heavy-laden, and clothe the naked" (275–76). The description of Heaven itself (171–271) owes much to Virgil's Elysian Fields in

the *Aeneid* and his Golden Age in the fourth eclogue, and more
to Dante's Earthly Paradise in the *Purgatorio*. Descriptions of the
locus amoenus, the "pleasant place," found in classical epic and pastoral had, of course, quite early supplied Christian poets with suggestions for their representations of Paradise.[4] Boccaccio's Paradise is a
pleasaunce beside a wooded mountain, with flowers, fruit trees, and
streams, where "gentle lions," and all other beasts and birds live
peacefully; perpetual spring reigns there, and death, disease, old age,
and want are unknown; the Almighty Shepherd Archesilaus bears in
his arms a lamb, and around them stand satyrs, who allegorically represent angels, crowned with wreaths of red roses and singing praises
to the lamb. Such eclogues are only marginally pastoral. However,
they stand as interesting testimonies to the humanists' determination
to absorb the whole world of pagan myth into the central truths of
Christian belief.

Boccaccio's eclogues were never as well known or influential as
Petrarch's, and by the time they were first printed in 1504 had been
overshadowed by the work of Giovanni Battista Spagnuoli (1448–
1516). Spagnuoli, known to posterity as Mantuanus—"the Mantuan"—
was an eminent clerical politician and an enormously fertile writer;
he wrote eight eclogues (ca. 1465), and two more to complete the
Virgilian number (ca. 1498), when all ten were first printed. The
first three are dialogues between Faustus and Fortunatus on the joys
of lawful married love and the pains of illicit passion, poems which
are saved from academism by Mantuan's realism and patronizing sense
of fun. Here is his description of the drunken bagpiper Tonius at
the rustic wedding in eclogue 1:

> With bag and drone and chanter then uprose
> The manly piper, with his manly pose:
> His head is raised aloft, with gesture grand,
> His cheeks empurpled swell, his lungs expand,
> His eyes protrude, his eyebrows rise and soar;
> He stamps his foot, and struts about the floor.[5]   (163–68)

Eclogue 4 is a savage and coarse denunciation of the nature of
woman, "servile genus, crudele, superbum": eclogue 5, similarly, takes
a Juvenalian theme, the behavior of patrons to poets. In eclogue 6
there is material more appropriate to a pastoral eclogue, with a

debate opposing life in the countryside to life in the city. The last three eclogues, however, are ecclesiastical allegories, which is no more than one would expect from a pastoralist of Mantuan's age and calling: in them, according to regular Renaissance fashion, he absorbs pagan myth into Christianity. In eclogue 7 a shepherd is warned in a vision to retire to Mount Carmel, that is, to join the Carmelite order. In eclogue 10 two shepherds representing two divisions of Carmelites debate various abuses in the order. Eclogue 9 is a vigorous satire upon abuses in the government of the church which was to provide generations of Protestant pastoralists, Spenser and Milton among them, with ammunition wherewith to attack the papacy. The world of Mantuan's shepherds, whether they are real peasants or allegorical Carmelite politicians, is not Arcadia: it is rather a metaphor of the trials, struggles, sorrows, and rare pleasures of real life, for Mantuan agrees with Boccaccio that the pastoral world can only be perfected in Heaven.

Throughout the sixteenth century Mantuan's eclogues were matched in popularity and influence only by Virgil's; indeed, they were adopted alongside Virgil's as school text books of Latin poetry and models for composition. The opening verse of "good old Mantuan's" first eclogue—"Facile precor gelida quando pecus omne sub umbra / Ruminat"—was a tag that every schoolboy knew when the dunce Holofernes misquoted it in *Love's Labour's Lost*.[6] Long passages from Mantuan's eclogues were closely imitated by Barclay, Spenser, and many other English writers of bucolic poetry, and an English translation by George Turbervile ran into four editions between 1567 and 1597.

Alongside Mantuan in the line of influential neo-Latin pastoral writers must be placed the figure of Jacopo Sannazaro (1456–1530) who, in retirement at his villa overlooking the Bay of Naples, wrote five fishermen's eclogues, *Eclogae Piscatoriae*, which were printed in 1526. The idea of a piscatorial eclogue was taken from the idylls of Theocritus, but the language is, as usual in the neo-Latin pastoral, self-consciously Virgilian. The merit of Sannazaro's eclogues lies in a fresh and gay inventiveness by which conventional themes, situations, and well-worn phrases of bucolic verse are adapted to the seaside settings, and by the affectionate sense of locality that informs the poet's description of these settings.

The Latin eclogue proliferated all over Europe in the sixteenth and seventeenth centuries, nowhere more tenaciously than upon the barren soil of Scotland.[7] Among English writers in this genre are Thomas Watson, Giles and Phineas Fletcher, and John Norris of Bemerton, though the finest English example of Latin pastoral is Milton's *Epitaphium Damonis*. Much ingenuity was spent by neo-Latinists in attempting to extend the scope of that Virgilian pastoral upon which all their work was based. Sailors, gardeners, vine-dressers, fishermen, and others joined the shepherds, while allegory was extended into every possible panegyrical, satirical, devotional, even liturgical purpose. However, perhaps the work only of Sannazaro and Milton deserves to escape W. W. Greg's blanket condemnation:

The latin eclogues of the renaissance are distinguished from all other forms of allegory by the obscure and recondite allusions that they affected. There were few among their authors for whom the narration of simple loves and sorrows or the graces of untutored nature possessed any attraction; we find them either making their shepherds openly discuss contemporary affairs, or more often clothing their references to actual events in a sort of pastoral allegory, fatuous as regards its form and obscure as regards its content.[8]

With Sannazaro this sketch of neo-Latin pastoral poetry must end, and with him begins the account of vernacular pastoral in the Renaissance. His *Arcadia*, written in Italian, mostly ca. 1483–85, and first printed piratically in 1502, appeared in a new edition on average every two years through the sixteenth century and diffused its influence widely. The work is a medley of twelve prose chapters interspersed with twelve verse eclogues, all strung upon a slight narrative thread. Sannazaro greatly expands that hint in the seventh eclogue of Virgil where Corydon and Thyrsis are spoken of as "Arcades ambo," and in doing so creates a whole region, a country of the mind.

The historical Arcadia of antiquity was known as the haunt of Pan, and its people were famed musicians, but their land was poor, bare, and rocky. Virgil first associated that region with luscious landscapes of pastoral art—flowered meadows, cool groves, mild breezes, and the rest—but it was left for Sannazaro to be the geographer of this imaginary land. The first prose section of his *Arcadia* opens with a splendid

set-piece description, some sixty lines long, where Sannazaro loads
every rift with ore. With exquisite and elaborate art he proclaims
his artlessness:

Songs carved on the rugged barks of beeches no less delight the one who
reads them than do learned verses written on the smooth pages of gilded
books. And the wax-bound reeds of shepherds proffer amid the flower-
laden valleys perhaps more pleasurable sound than do through proud
chambers the polished and costly boxwood instruments of the musicians.
And who has any doubt that a fountain that issues naturally from the
living rock, surrounded by green growth, is more pleasing to the human
mind than all the others made by art of whitest marble, resplendent with
much gold? Certainly no one, to my thinking. Therefore relying on that,
I shall among these deserted places recount to the listening trees, and
to those shepherds that will be there, the rude eclogues issued from a
natural vein, setting them forth just as naked of ornament as I heard
them sung by the shepherds of Arcady under the delightful shades, to
the murmuring of crystal fountains. To whom not one time but a
thousand the mountain Deities overcome by sweetness lent their listening ears, and the delicate Nymphs, forgetful of pursuing the wandering
beasts, abandoned quiver and bow at the foot of the towering pines of
Maenalus and of Lycaeus. Wherefore I, if it were permitted me, would
think it more glorious to set my mouth to the lowly pipe of Corydon,
given him long ago as a precious gift from Damoetas, than to the sound-
ing flute of Pallas, with which the unhappily prideful Satyr provoked
Apollo, to his own misfortune. (prologue)[9]

Arcadia is nature idealized, but, as frequent allusions to classical pastoral reveal, this mythical land also represents the perfection of art.

   There is hardly any sequential narrative in the *Arcadia*; the reader
is invited merely to linger in a landscape of fragile and unearthly
beauty. What unity Sannazaro's work possesses is supplied by the
figure of the courtier in retirement, Sincero, who has fled from Naples
in order to forget his obdurate mistress, but who cannot help remem-
bering her wherever he wanders in Arcadia. His love-laments are
echoed by Arcadian shepherds, two of whom sing, in the fourth eclogue, a double sestina which was to provide a model for Sidney's
splendid exercise in this form (see chap. 4). In his fifth eclogue
Virgil had raised a tomb in the ideal landscape of pastoral; Sannazaro
raises three in his *Arcadia*. The third, in eclogue 12, probably supplied
Poussin with the hint for his painting in the Louvre, *Et in Arcadia*

ego, from which stemmed a highly fruitful literary and iconographic tradition.[10]

Pastoral spread westward into Spain, where pastoral romance was brought to a high pitch of art in Montemayor's *Diana* (ca. 1560), and Cervantes's *Galatea* (1584); and northward into France, where Clement Marot wrote in 1531 a pastoral elegy upon Loyse de Savoye which would later be read with some profit by Spenser. In England the first writer of formal pastoral eclogues in the vernacular was the priest Alexander Barclay (1476–1552). At unknown dates, probably in the second decade of the sixteenth century, he wrote five eclogues[11] whose average length is over a thousand verses. The first three, in Barclay's words, "conteyne the miseryes of Courtiers and Courtes of all princes in generall, Gathered out of a booke named in Latin, MISERIAE CURIALIUM, compiled by Eneas Syluius Poet and Oratour." Aeneas Sylvius Piccolomini (1405–64), the orator and diplomat who rose to become Pope Pius II, composed his Latin treatise *Miseriae Curialium* to denounce the ambition, greed, and vice of courtiers. Barclay adheres closely to his model and arrives at the expected conclusion "Poore life is surest, the court is but torment."

These three eclogues contain several passages of translation from the standard Renaissance pastoral model, Mantuan. Barclay's fifth eclogue, "of the disputation of Citizens and men of the Countrey," is a close imitation of Mantuan's sixth, while Barclay's fourth, "treating of the behaviour of rich men agaynst Poetes," is a zestful adaptation of Mantuan's fifth. Like Mantuan, Barclay envies Tityrus (Virgil) in his enjoyment of the patronage of Maecenas, but his own appeal for patronage is distinctly earthy, and significantly brings the English country house ideal into pastoral (cf. chap. 7):

> A plentifull house out chaseth thought and care,
> Sojourne doth sorowe there where all thing is bare,
> The seller couched with bere, with ale or wine,
> The meates ready when man hath lust to dine.
> Great barnes full, fat wethers in the folde,
> The purse well stuffed with silver and with golde. (391–96)

Barclay's verse is rough and inordinately prolix. In his prologue he apologizes for his "lack of eloquence": "It were not fitting a heard or man rurall / To speake in terms gay and rhetoricall" (83–84). His style is decorously "low," but, after the customary Renais-

sance fashion, his matter is court-and-church compliment and satire
(including a few satiric hits in the fourth eclogue against the poet-
laureate Skelton). Occasionally real country life can be seen, and
Barclay's Corvix, introduced in the first eclogue, has the appearance
of a poor English country fellow in his Kendal Green, and rough,
high-laced boots ("cockers"), with his wooden spoon stuck in the
side of his felt hat:

> At divers holes his heare grewe through his hode,
> A stiffe patched felt hanging over his eyne,
> His costly clothing was thredebare kendall grene,
> His patched cockers skant reached to his knee,
> In the side of his felte there stacke a spone of tree,
> A botle his cote on the one side had torne.   (146–51)

Barclay's eclogues were separately printed at various unknown dates
before they were first collected in 1570, but had little influence on
English writers of pastoral in the sixteenth century. Mantuan remained the prime model. His satirical eclogues were paraphrased and
vigorously Puritanized in Barnabe Googe's *Eglogs* (1563).[12] Thus
Googe in eclogue 3 on the Marian persecutions:

> Such Shepe, as would not them obaye
>   but in theyr Pasture byde,
> With (cruell flames,) they did consume
>   and vex on every syde.
> And with the shepe, ye Shepherdes good,
>   (O hate full Hounds of Hell,)
> They did torment, and dryve them out,
>   in Places farre to dwell.   (53–56)

Googe's trotting "fourteeners" do not make a happy English counterpart to classical and neo-Latin hexameters, but George Turberville
used fourteeners also for his translation into English (1567)[13] of the
first nine of the Mantuan's eclogues.

Chapter Four

Spenser and Sidney

Barclay, Googe, and Turbervile mark the extent of the English pastoral eclogue before 1579. Thus, there was very little to anticipate the publication of Spenser's *The Shepheardes Calender*, the most ambitious and artful of all English eclogue collections, before or since that year. In this work Spenser draws together several traditions, and his eclogues perform all the major functions that earlier pastorals fulfilled.[1] The most remarkable feature, however, is the great metrical and linguistic virtuosity: Spenser uses Barclayan roughness and colloquialism for the "low" matter of topical political and ecclesiastical satire, but elsewhere, in deliberate and masterly contrast, he employs a considerable range of complex but fluent lyrical measures.[2]

From its very first appearance *The Shepheardes Calender* was accompanied by the kind of *apparatus criticus* that was appropriate to a literary classic. It was, indeed, the first English poem to receive this distinction. Annotation is supplied by one E. K., whose dedicatory epistle and laborious *scholia* mingle an awe-inspiring, solemn, pedantic, supererogatory fatuity with critical acuteness. Many of his textual glosses explain the allegory—for Spenser, like Petrarch, requires his key—while others appear to be intended to divert the reader's attention from possibility seditious implications of allusions to contemporary politics.[3] Particularly useful is E. K.'s division of the twelve eclogues into three kinds: plaintive (*Januarye, June, November*, and *December*), moral "which for the most part be mixed with some Satyrical bitternesse" (*Februarie, Maye, Julye, September*, and *October*), and recreative (*March, Aprill*, and *August*). The five "moral" eclogues are debates in which one shepherd adopts an austere, moralistic view, as Piers does when he calls for otherworldliness in the

priesthood (*Maye*) or the craft of poetry (*October*), while another
shepherd takes a freer, easier attitude, as Cuddie does in asserting
the impatient sexuality of youth (*Februarie*) or allowing that the
poet must take account of practical necessity (*October*).[4] In the other
eclogues, plaintive or recreative, love, as a source of pleasure but
more often a source of pain, is the dominant theme.

The series begins with a plaintive eclogue. The first two stanzas
of *Januarye* and the last describe Colin Clout bringing his winter-
beaten flock out for a short afternoon in the field and then returning
them to the fold. This provides a pastoral and seasonal setting for
the shepherd's complaint of unrequited love (ten stanzas long) which
occupies most of the poem. The structure of the eclogue, then, is
Theocritean, and the pathetic fallacy is introduced, but in a mood
very different from Theocritus's. For Colin the wintry landscape
reflects the despair in his heart: "Thou barrein ground, whome win-
ters wrath hath wasted / Art made a myrrhour, to behold my plight"
(19–20);[5] and the mirror images duly follow:

> You naked trees, whose shady leaves are lost,
> Wherein the byrds were wont to build their bowre:
> And now are clothd with mosse and hoary frost,
> Instede of bloosmes, wherewith your buds did flowre:
> I see your teares, that from your boughs doe raine,
> Whose drops in drery ysicles remaine.
>
> All so my lustfull leafe is drye and sere,
> My timely buds with wayling all are wasted:
> The blossome, which my braunch of youth did beare,
> With breathed sighes is blown away, and blasted,
> And from mine eyes the drizling teares descend,
> As on your boughes the ysicles depend.   (31–42)

"Colin Clout" was John Skelton's pseudonym in his role of rough,
antiprelatic satirist, and Spenser adopts the name as a persona here,
as too in *Colin Clouts Come Home Againe* and *The Faerie Queene*,
book 6, canto 10.

The "set-piece" which forms the core of *Februarie* is not a lyric,
but the moral fable of the Briar and the Oak (lines 102–238),
recounted by an aged shepherd Thenot in an unsuccessful attempt to
convince a young shepherd, Cuddie, of the respect due to age. The

style is rough and the language obtrusively "archaic" in the Chaucerian manner, for we are told that the fable was learned from "Thyrsis" (that is, Chaucer). Cuddie's retort to Thenot's homily certainly recaptures the tones of Chaucer's Host, or any "real" shepherd:

> Now I pray thee shepherd, tel it not forth:
> Here is a long tale, and little worth.
> So longe have I listened to thy speche,
> That graffed to the gound is my breche. (239–42)

The last line—"Hye thee home shepherd, the day is nigh wasted"—supplies the conventional Virgilian eclogue ending, but also, in reminding us that Thenot is very old and must die soon, it touches the theme of time's decay that runs through *The Shepheardes Calender.*

The rough humor at the close of *Februarie* prepares the reader for the central set-piece (61–102) in *March*, where a blundering young fowler, Thomalin, tells how he shot arrows at Cupid and pelted him with pumice-stones before the love-god shot him in the heel. This fable of nascent eroticism[6] is taken from Bion with hints from Ronsard, but in Spenser the encounter between this ill-matched pair of huntsmen makes a lively little comedy, versified, appropriately enough, in the metre of Chaucer's *Sir Thopas.*

Very different is the set-piece (37–153) that occupies the greater part of *Aprill*, Colin Clout's hymn in praise "Of fayre Elisa, Queene of Shepheardes all," which is couched in an intricate and skillfully handled lyric stanza. In this gorgeous panegyric Queen Elizabeth is shown as attended by the Muses and the Graces, and as shaming Phoebus and Cynthia with her beauty. She is adorned with all the splendors of art and nature, and garlanded with flowers of every season, for she is queen of an undecaying ideal realm which enjoys a golden age and is unaffected by seasonal change:

> See, where she sits upon the grassie greene,
>   (O seemely sight)
> Yclad in Scarlot like a mayden Queene,
>   And Ermines white,
> Upon her head a Cremosin coronet,
> With Damaske roses and Daffadillies set:

> Bayleaves between,
> And Primroses greene
> Embellish the sweete Violet.   (55–63)

The introductory and brief concluding dialogues that provide a conventional pastoral "frame" for this piece of rhetorical and metrical
virtuosity are in a deliberately contrasting plain style.

For the principal episode in *Maye* Spenser returns to the Aesopian
type of fable employed in *Februarie*. The story of the Fox and the
Kid (174–305) is a homiletic allegory concerning the crafty wicked
pastor who devours his charge, and forms the climax of the stern
Puritan Piers's argument against Palinode, the morally lax Anglican
priest. Spenser's malcontent allegory maintains its pastoral character
tolerably well; for instance, an image of the corrupt sheepmaster
and shepherd serves appropriately enough to attack absentee purchas-
ers and cynical vendors of benefices:

> But they bene hyred for little pay
>   Of other, that caren as little as they,
>   What fallen the flocke, so they han the fleece....
>   I muse, what account both these will make ...
>   When great *Pan* account of Shepherdes shall aske.   (47–54)

This eclogue is very obviously in the medieval tradition of Christianized allegorical pastoral, as E. K.'s gloss makes clear: "*Great Pan*
is Christ, the very God of all shepheards, which calleth himselfe
the greate and good shepheard. The name is most rightly (me thinkes)
applied to him, for Pan signifieth all, or omnipotent, which is onely
the Lord Jesus."

From the shepherd as Christian pastor, Spenser turns in *June* to
the shepherd as poet, and the unhappy Colin Clout returns in person
to lament his ill success in love, and to voice his fears that his poetic
powers are waning. His complaint (65–112) grows out of a dialogue
with his contented friend Hobbinol whose mood is in tune with the
delicious surrounding landscape of gently falling waters, cool shade,
flowery glade, gentle breezes, and singing birds. In Hobbinol's song
there are echoes of Virgil's first eclogue, where the happy ease and
security of Tityrus is contrasted with Meliboeus's misery; but in
Spenser's eclogue the figures of classical mythology are "naturalized"

alongside the objects of English rural superstition. Hobbinol invites
Colin to the sweet vales where

> ... friendly faeries, met with many Graces,
> And lightfote Nymphes can chase the lingring night,
> With Heydeguyes [i.e., dances], and trimly trodden traces,
> Whilst systers nyne, which dwell on *Parnasse* hight
> Doe make them musick, for their more delight.   (25–29)

According to the envious Colin, Hobbinol has found the Paradise
which Adam lost, but Colin, as in *Januarye* and *December*, carries
winter in his heart, and is exiled from that timeless Eden.

Continuing his alternation of lyrical sweetness with Barclayan
satirical roughness, Spenser uses the jog-trot measure of the divided
"fourteener" to present in *Julye* a debate between the Puritan "good
shepehearde" on the lowly plain and the "proude and ambitious Pas-
tour" upon the hill. This debate is based in a general way upon
Mantuan's eighth eclogue and is linked with Spenser's own *Maye*.
The allegory is transparent and the pastoral mask carried perfunctorily:
thus Thomalin reports that at Rome shepherds behave like lords:

> Theyr sheepe han crustes, and they the bread:
>   the chippes, and they the chere:
> They han the fleece, and eke the flesh,
>   (O seely sheepe the while)
> The corne is theyrs, let other thresh,
>   their hands they may not file.   (187–92)

Such writing represents a perversion and a considerable narrowing of
the pastoral mode that Theocritus and Virgil had created.

August takes the Theocritean-Virgilian framework of a singing
match. There is a charmingly impromptu air to the contest (53–124)
between Perigot who sings of his love-longing and Willie who caps
each verse with a mocking echo or reply:

> Per. And if for gracelesse greefe I dye,
> Wil. hey ho gracelesse griefe,
> Per. Witnesse, shee slewe me with here eye:
> Wil. let thy follye be the priefe.

Before Spenser's day, there was a popular song tune called "Heigh
ho holiday"—it is the tune to which, for instance, "A pastoral song"
in Thomas Deloney's *Garland of Good Will* was intended to be
sung—and the rough and simple roundelay sung by Willie and
Perigot is probably based on that tune. After such homely gaiety
there is a complete contrast when the umpire Cuddie sings a song
by Colin Clout (151–89) which employs the complicated Italian
sestina form to lament more earnestly the pains of unrequited love.
Each song is appropriate to its singer; and together they embrace
two streams of pastoral art, English and European, and two moods,
spontaneous and reflective.

September is the most bitter of Spenser's several attacks upon
evil pastors. His model here is Mantuan's ninth eclogue, itself a
satirical adaptation of Virgil's first, and, as in Mantuan, the text is
Matthew 7:15: "Beware of false prophets, which come to you in
sheep's clothing, but inwardly they are ravening wolves" (A.V.).

October is couched in an altogether higher style; again the character of the shepherd changes from pastor to poet. Cuddie, in a dialogue
with Piers, utters the old lament, heard in Theocritus's (nonpastoral)
idyll 16, that the patrons for poets and the high subjects for verse
have all disappeared:

> But ah *Mecoenas* is yclad in claye,
> And great *Augustus* long ygoe is dead:
> And all the worthies liggen wrapt in leade
> That matter made for Poets on to play.   (61–64)

Poetry has its uses to feed youth's fancy (line 14), to be a moral
force in the affairs of men (21–24), or to embody patriotic ideas
(39–48), but in its highest form its value is its holiness as a divine
gift (83–84). Near the end of the eclogue Colin's case is adduced:
Cuddie claims that were Colin not disabled by unhappy love he would
"mount as high, and sing as soote as Swanne," but Piers replies that
Colin is foolish because he does not comprehend that

> . . . love does teach him climbe so hie,
> And lyftes him up out of the loathsome myre:
> Such immortall mirrhor, as he doth admire,
> Would rayse ones mynd above the starry skie.   (91–94)

From the beginning with Theocritus, carnal or sentimental love had been principal motifs of pastoral. Spenser here brings into the eclogue tradition the notion of Platonic love that he was to elaborate later in his own *Fowre Hymnes*.

The lyrical centerpiece of *November* is the elaborate elegy for an unidentified Dido (52–202), sung by Colin Clout in a flexible and fluid measure, which outdoes in melodic variety even the song in *Aprill*. The immediate model is Clement Marot's *De Madame Loyse*, but the most effective devices in both Marot and Spenser go back to the Lament for Bion or to Virgil's fifth eclogue. These devices include the poignant commonplace that the individual man must die while flowers are renewed every springtime (83–92), the pathetic fallacy that all nature mourns (123–42), the sudden "turn" to hope (163–72), and the triumphant assertion that "she is not dead." As Virgil's Daphnis had become a god, so Dido

> …raignes a goddesse now emong the saintes,
> That whilome was the saynt of shepheards light:
> And is enstalled nowe in heavens hight. (175–77)

In *December* (partly modeled on Marot's *Eclogue au Roy*) the year ends with a plaintive monologue in which Colin, using the same stanza as in *Januarye*, sums up the course of his life and compares it to the four seasons. His springtime was full of the glad animal joys of boyhood, "Like Swallow swift I wandred here and there" (20), when he seemed to live in a timeless world. Summer brought the full growth of his poet's skill, but brought also unhappiness in love. In Autumn his harvest was of unfulfilled hopes. Now: "Winter is come, that blowes the balefull breath, / And after Winter commeth timely death" (149–50).

Thus the *Calender* ends as it had begun, with the solitary figure of the disappointed shepherd-poet singing to himself. The dominant mood of the series of eclogues is melancholy. There is more sorrow than anger in the satirical eclogues, and even the panegyric to Elisa is set within a shepherd dialogue which refers to Colin's sorrows. In *December*, and in the formal scheme of the entire *Calender*, Spenser, in Pope's words, "compares human Life to the several Seasons, and at once exposes to his readers a view of the great and little worlds, in their various changes and aspects,"[7] but the unity provided by the figure of Colin Clout does more than this. Spenser's creation of this melancholy lover and poet, who is at once the inhabitant and the creator of an imagined world mysteriously distinct from and yet vitally related to our own, is an expression of artistic self-consciousness, richer than anything in Virgil and unattempted by Theocritus.

In one respect, however, Spenser is closer to Theocritus than to Virgil. In Virgil and in most medieval Latin pastoral there was no linguistic equivalent to Theocritus's Doric, but one of Spenser's most remarkable achievements was to fashion such an equivalent, a language which appeared rustic and yet was sufficiently artful and resourceful to be the poetic vehicle of serious matter. His "English Doric" is deeply rooted in native poetic traditions, drawing as it does upon the language of Chaucer the court poet, Langland the moralist, and Skelton the satirist.

Spenser found that the pastoral mask sat well upon him. In the character of a shepherd he sang his pensive dirge *Daphnaida* (1596) upon the death of Lady Douglas Howard; while his *Astrophel, A Pastorall Elegie upon the death of the most Noble and Valorous Knight, Sir Philip Sidney*, mourned its subject as a "gentle shepherd borne in Arcady." This title appears to have been the earliest recorded use of the term "pastoral elegy" in English. The poem uses the ancient pastoral matter of the Adonis story, though Spenser's handling of the myth owes less to Bion directly than it does to Ronsard's *Adonis* (1563). *Astrophel* forms an introduction or narrative frame, almost in the fashion of a pastoral eclogue, to *The Dolefull Lay of Clorinda* sung by the dead Astrophel's shepherdess sister (that is, Spenser here attributes a poem of his own composition to Sidney's sister and his own patroness, the Countess of Pembroke). These poems may well have been written fairly soon after Sidney's death in 1586, but they were not printed until 1595 when they were published as an appendix to *Colin Clouts Come Home Againe*. This work of 955 lines, Spenser's longest eclogue, tells of Colin's journey to court at the invitation of the "Shepherd of the Ocean," that is, Ralegh, and his disillusioned return home. Most of the poem is a highly laudatory account of the glories of the Court of Cynthia, i.e., Queen Elizabeth; but when Colin's fellow shepherds ask why he left such splendors to return to rustic life, he launches into a denunciation of the ambition, treachery, extravagance, vanity, and folly of courtiers. Colin, or Spenser, hardly attempts to resolve the contradiction between his ambition to be a court poet singing Cynthia's praise, and his conventional moral disapproval of court as contrasted with country.

Colin Clout's final appearance is in the last completed book of *The Faerie Queene*, when Sir Calidore, attracted by the beauty of Pastorella as much as by Meliboee's account of the joys and virtues of the humble shepherd's life, plays truant from the quest laid upon him by Gloriana. Colin is the shepherd whose rural piping and gay caroling are esteemed by Pastorella above the courtly lays of Calidore. Then in the strange and beautiful climax of the book (canto 10, stanzas 11–16) he pipes on Mount Acidale to the dance of the Graces themselves—"the daughters of delight" who are the divine source of beauty in human life:

> These three on men all gracious gifts bestow,
> Which decke the body or adorne the mynde,
> To make them lovely or well favoured show.   (stanza 23)

In the center of them the shepherd-lover places his own mistress as his source of grace. For the shepherd-poet the dance of the Graces represents the harmony of an ideal imaginative order. Only the poet's art, indeed, can bring this vision of the ideal world of the imagination into the tangible world of natural appearances. The vision is fragile, and Calidore's interruption dispels it. The world of pastoral peace is correspondingly fragile; a little later the Brigants break in, kill Meliboee and his wife and carry off Pastorella, and Calidore, willy-nilly, returns to the hard paths of his chivalric quest.[8]

The contrast in *The Faerie Queene*, book 6, between the life of heroic endeavor and that of pastoral retirement is no less explicit in Sidney's *Arcadia*, written in 1580.[9] Despite its title and its derivation (through Montemayor's *Diana*) from Sannazaro's *Arcadia*, Sidney's work is more of a chivalric epic than an Arcadian romance. The prose that constitutes the greater part of Sidney's *Arcadia* lies, in any case, outside the scope of this study, but any history of pastoral poetry needs to take some account of the four groups of eclogues which divide the prose narrative into what Sidney himself called five "acts." These groups contain altogether twenty-seven poems in a great variety of meters, totaling 2,500 lines, and thus constitute an eclogue series as long as *The Shepheardes Calender*. Songs or fables in each group are gathered loosely around a single theme, and these themes form a natural progression. The first treats of the sorrows of unrequited love, the second the struggle between reason and passion in the soul of the lover, the third presents married love (and includes the first formal epithalamium in English), and the fourth death, with yet one more adaptation of the *Lament for Bion*—whose influence reached Sidney by way of the eleventh eclogue in Sannazaro's *Arcadia*.

The main narrative of the *Arcadia* concerns princes in rural retirement, and over half of the songs in these eclogue-interludes are put into the mouths of courtiers disguised as shepherds. Of these the most assigned to one character—five—are sung by Philisides, who also sings two more songs in the main body of the *Arcadia*. His name is made up of the first syllables of Sidney's names, and, since it signifies star-lover, it parallels Sidney's persona in his *Astrophil and Stella*. The melancholy Philisides drifts through the *Arcadia* lamenting his unhappiness in love and, at last, in *The Fourth Eclogues* he is prevailed upon to tell his life-story in prose and verse, a story which corresponds at many points with the history of Sidney's own early life. Earlier, in the fourth poem of *The Third Eclogues*, Philisides had recited a fable, embodying a political allegory, which, one August, "old Languet had me taught, / Languet, the shepherd best swift Ister, knew"[10] (22–23). Sidney toured the continent under Hubert Languet's tutelage and they were together in Vienna on the Danube (Ister) in August 1573 and 1574. Thus in the character of Philisides, even more obviously than in Spenser's Colin Clout, a shepherd is the fictionalized self-portrait of his creator. Sidney, however, later became dissatisfied with much of this allegorical autobiography, and in his revisions for the version of the *Arcadia* published posthumously in 1590 he reassigned or omitted Philisides' songs, though his name is retained and allocated to an Iberian knight who appears once only and is known as the lover of a star—Stella.

Most of the eclogues are characterized by the moral earnestness of the whole *Arcadia*, but there are occasional attempts at a lighter touch. The second poem of *The Third Eclogues* is a comic fabliau. The third poem of *The Second Eclogues*—a song contest between two rustics, Nico and Pas—derives from Theocritus's fifth idyll and Virgil's third eclogue; but Sidney's touches of burlesque are, by comparison with his masters', very heavy-handed. The other poems in *The Second Eclogues* are more characteristic of Sidney's mind and art. The first in the group is an antiphonal chorus of Arcadians singing to accompany a dance which they called the skirmish betwixt Reason and Passion. For seven shepherds which were named the reasonable shepherds joined themselves, four of them making a square and other two going a little wide of either side, like wings for the main battle, and the seventh man foremost, like the forlorn hope, to begin the skirmish. In like order came out the seven apassionate shepherds, all keeping the pace of their foot by their voice and sundry consorted instruments they held in their arms.

Renaissance pastoral readily absorbed the materials of allegorical pageant, as such works as Sidney's own pastoral entertainment for Queen Elizabeth, *The Lady of May* (written 1578), had shown, and as the masque was later to show.

Other poems in *The Second Eclogues* experiment with quantitative meters, and one, sung by the melancholy Philisides, exploits the echo device that had been used by Ovid in his story of Narcissus and Echo (*Metamorphoses*, bk. 3, ll. 379–92). The last poem in the group is sung by the prince Musidorus disguised as a shepherd and begins:

> O sweet woods, the delight of solitariness!
> O how much I do like your solitariness!
> Where man's mind hath a freed consideration
> Of goodness to receive lovely direction;
> Where senses do behold th'order of heav'nly host,
> And wise thoughts do behold what the creator is.
> Contemplation here holdeth his only seat,
> Bounded with no limits, borne with a wing of hope,
> Climbs even unto the stars; Nature is under it. (1–9)

The struggle between reason and passion has come to an end; and here, in serenity of mind, Musidorus praises rural solitude that lifts man's thoughts to heaven.

Sidney's metrical virtuosity is not seen to uniformly happy effect in the *Arcadia* eclogues, but one undoubted success is the double sestina—"an exotic without progeny"[11]—sung at the beginning of *The Fourth Eclogues* by Strephon and Klaius, two courtiers turned shepherds. In this wonderfully artful poem the same six line endings are used in every stanza, but in revolving order, so that for six stanzas each one of the words ends a different line in each stanza, and so that the last word of one stanza is always repeated at the end of the first line of the following stanza. Then the pattern of line endings is exactly repeated for six more stanzas. Finally the six words are repeated in the course of a concluding tercet. This song is modeled on the fourth eclogue in Sannazaro's *Arcadia*, a double sestina in which the verse-endings are "campi" ("fields"), "sassi" ("rocks"), "valle" ("valley"), "rime" ("verse"), "pianto" ("lament") and "giorno" ("day"). Sidney's line endings, "mountains," "vallies," "forests," "music," "morning," "evening," correspond closely. In both cases the first three represent recurrent landmarks and the last three a daily repetition of complaint: together they insist that the pastoral landscape is a closed world of love-longing. The double sestina form has the insistent mathematical regularity in variety of a change-ringing of bells. William Empson writes:

This form has no direction or momentum; it beats, however rich its orchestration, with a wailing and immovable monotony, for ever upon the same doors in vain. *Mountaines, vallies, forrests; musique, morning, evening*; it is at these words only that Klaius and Strephon pause in their cries; these words circumscribe their world; these are the bones of their situation; and in tracing their lovelorn pastoral tedium through thirteen repetitions, with something of the aimless multitudinous beating of the sea on a rock, we seem to extract all the meaning possible from these notions.[12]

What begins as one conventional lover's complaint, capped and expanded by another's, develops into a nightmare vision of a world turned topsy-turvy by the effects of their unhappiness:

> *Strephon.*   Meseems I see the high and stately mountains
> Transform themselves to low dejected valleys.
> Meseems I hear in these ill-changed forests
> The nightingales do learn of owls their music.
> Meseems I feel the comfort of the morning
> Turned to the mortal serene of an evening.
> *Klaius.*   Meseems I see a filthy cloudy evening
> As soon as sun begins to climb the mountains.
> Meseems I feel a noisome scent the morning
> When I do smell the flowers of these valleys.
> Meseems I hear (when I do hear sweete music)
> The dreadful cries of murdered men in forests.   (37–48)

The reason for Strephon and Klaius's sorrow is that Urania, Heavenly Love, has left them; and something of their sad history is recounted by the shepherd Lamon in a lengthy but incomplete song (544 lines) added to the end of *The First Eclogues* in the revised version of the *Arcadia* printed in 1593. This narrative is an uncompleted allegory of Platonic love. The shepherds at first enjoy the simple animal joys of youth, much as Colin Clout in his springtime: their sorrows and their spiritual growth begin with the advent of Urania (Heavenly Love), whose beauty outshines that of the other two shepherdesses, Nous (Intellectual Love), and Cosma (Bodily Love). The progress of the shepherds' affections is traced symbolically through the course of a game of barley break[13] at a village festival where Strephon changes partners from Urania to sturdy Cosma, to dainty Nous, and back to radiant Urania again. "Thus Strephon, in all his pastoral innocence, mimes out the descent of the soul, its refusal of the created cosmos of matter and of the divine world of Ideas for something higher like union with the One to which Urania or Heavenly Love may lead him."[14] This neo-Platonic allegory does not sit too incongruously upon what is a quite lively sketch of rustic merrymaking.

For both Sidney and Spenser pastoral eclogue was primarily a vehicle for allegory, and this was the common view of Elizabethan critics. E. K. declared of Spenser in the dedicatory epistle to *The Shepherdes Calender*: "He chose rather to unfold great matter of argument covertly . . . which moved him rather in Aeglogues, then other wise to write." George Puttenham, ten years later, made the same point concerning poets in general: "the poet devised the Eglogue . . . not of purpose to counterfeit or represent the rustical manner of loves and communication: but under the vaile of homely persons, and in rude speeches to insinuate and glaunce at greater matters."[15]

Chapter Five

Some Spenserians

Allegory became a less potent lure as Elizabethan and Jacobean poets moved further away from Italian models. A late Jacobean critic, Michael Drayton, in the address to the reader of his *Pastorals* (1619), admits allegory as a possibility rather than a necessity: "the most High, and most Noble Matters of the World may bee shaddowed in them, and for certaine sometimes are." However, Drayton agrees with his predecessors that among English pastoral poets Spenser stands first: "Master Edmund Spenser had done enough for the immortality of his Name, had he only given us his Shepheards Kalender, a Master-piece if any."[1]

The Shepheardes Calender became the principal model for Elizabethan and Jacobean pastoral eclogue, although English translations from both Theocritus and Virgil appeared in the decade following its publication. *Six Idillia, that is, six small, or petty, poems, or aeglogues,* printed at Oxford in 1588 contained translations by an anonymous hand of idylls 8, 11, 16, 18, 20, and 31 attributed to Theocritus. The first four of these were discussed in chapter 1. Idyll 20, wrongly numbered 21 in the 1588 volume, is a pseudo-Theocritean piece in which an oxherd complains about Eunica, a girl in the town, who has rejected his love; he calls his fellow herdsmen to witness that he is handsome and accomplished, and regrets that Eunica is apparently unaware that even godddesses have loved country lads. Idyll 31 is a whimsical fable, according to which Aphrodite summons the boar which killed her beloved Adonis, and the creature explains that he had intended only to kiss the youth's naked thigh and had gored him by mistake. On this, Aphrodite forgives the boar and makes it one of her followers. The "Argument" prefixed by the translator in the 1588 edition displays that common Elizabethan tendency to

48

impose allegorical interpretations upon classical myth, for it concludes "The Poet's drift is to shew the power of Love, not only in men, but also in brute beasts: although in the last two verses, by the burning of the Boar's amorous teeth, he intimateth that extravagant and unorderly passions are to be restrained by reason."[2]

In 1591 appeared *The Shepherds Starre*, a much amplified "paraphrase upon the third of the Canticles of Theocritus, Dialogue wise" by Thomas Bradshaw; and in 1647 and 1651 translations by Thomas Stanley of idylls 20 and 31, and pieces by Bion and Moschus were published. Clearly, early translators went to the lightest and "prettiest" parts of Theocritus. The publication of a full translation had to wait until Thomas Creech's *Idylliums* (1684).

In the case of Virgil, William Webbe Englished the first and second eclogues in his *Discourse on English Poetry* (1596), and A. F. (possibly Abraham Fraunce) published in 1589 his translation of *The Bucoliks of P. Virgilius Maro . . . with his Georgiks*. Typical of his age, A. F. stressed the allegorical character of Virgil's eclogues: in the dedication he went so far as to claim that the "principall occasion of writing these Pastoralls was the majestie of *Julius Caesar* and *Augustus his sonne.*"

All types of formal eclogue represented in *The Shepheardes Calender* are found in the work of Spenser's Elizabethan and Jacobean successors, but love-complaint is the commonest. Virgil's pederastic second eclogue provided a model for the two opening poems of Richard Barnfield's *The Affectionate Shepherd* (1594): "The Tears of an Affectionate Shepheard sicke for Love or The Complaint of Daphnis for the Love of Ganimede," and "The Second Dayes Lamentation of The Affectionate Shepheard." Daphnis's invitation to love is accompanied by an offer of gifts, which include "Straw-berries or Bil-berries . . . Bath'd in a melting Sugar-Candie streame," " A golden Racket, and a Tennis-Ball," "a green Hat and a Feather," a lamb, a goat, a nightingale, green-cheese, nutmeg, ginger, and much else besides. All this goes back, through Virgil, to the less extravagantly miscellaneous catalog of gifts in the eleventh idyll of Theocritus. Theocritus's Polyphemus describes Galatea as "Whiter to look upon than curds, more delicate than a lamb, / Than a young calf more skittish, plumper than ripening grape," (20–21), and leaves it at that; Virgil does not elaborate on the beauty of Alexis which is simply announced in the first word of the eclogue, "formosum"; but Barnfield's Daphnis offers elaborate and luscious descriptions of the beautiful, unloving Ganimede:

> a sweet-fac'd Boy,
> (Whose amber locks trust up in golden tramels
> Dangle adowne his lovely cheekes with joy,
> When pearle and flowers his faire haire enamels)....
>
> His Ivory-white and Alabaster skin
> Is stained throughout with rare Vermillion red,
> Whose twinckling starrie lights do never blin
> To shine on lovely *Venus* (Beauties bed:)
>   But as the Lillie and the blushing Rose,
>   So white and red on him in order growes.[3]   (7–10, 13–18)

Barnfield's enameled and sugary elaboration of the catalog of gifts, and, more particularly, of the beauties of the reluctant boy clearly show the influence of recent erotic Ovidian mythological narrative poems by Lodge, Marlowe, and Shakespeare.

The third poem in Barnfield's volume, "The Shepherds Content, or The happines of a harmless life," conventionally compares the shepherd's life with the monarch's, courtier's, soldier's, scholar's, merchant's, and husbandman's. Though Barnfield's conception of the shepherd's life is Arcadian, he introduces frolics and well-known songs and dances of the English shepherd who,

> when Night comes drawes homeward to his Coate,
> Singing a Jigge or merry Roundelay;
> (For who sings commonly so merry a Noate,
> As he that cannot chop or change a groate)
>   And in the winter Nights (his chiefe desire)
>   He turns a Crabbe or Cracknell in the fire.
>
> He leads his Wench a Country Horn-pipe Round,
> About a May-pole on a Holy-day;
> Kissing his lovely Lasse (with Garlands Crownd)
> With whopping heigh-ho singing Care away.   (188–97)

Typical of Barnfield's eclecticism, this poem finds room for a love lament, an elegy on Sidney, and compliments to Spenser, Drayton, and

Watson (or his translator Fraunce), under their pastoral names of Colin, Rowland, and Amintas. Elizabethan pastoral of courtly compliment readily took up the Spenser-Sidney image of Elizabeth as queen of shepherds and lady of May. A funeral eclogue on Walsingham, *Meliboeus* (1590), translated by Thomas Watson from his own Latin, is by no means the only poem in which she is "Diana matchlesse Queene of Arcadie." In George Peele's thoroughly Spenserian *An Eglogue Gratulatorie* (1589), to "the right honourable and renowned Shepherd of Albions Arcadia," Robert earl of Essex, she is the employer of two swains, Sidney and Essex, who "served, and watch'd, and waited late, / To keep the grim wolf from Eliza's gate." Here the overtones of religious pastoral can be heard, for the grim wolf is not merely Spain but also Roman Catholicism, which threatens the innocent and peaceable flock of a queen who is supreme head of a national church. In 1603 Henry Chettle used eclogues and prose passages after the fashion of Sannazaro to weave a capacious *Englandes Mourning Garment*: "Worne here by plaine Shepheardes; in memorie of their sacred Mistresses, Elizabeth, Queen of Vertue while shee lived, and Theame of Sorrow, being dead. To which is added the true manner of her Emperiall Funerall. After which followeth the Shepheards Spring-Song, for entertainment of King James our most potent Soveraigne. Dedicated to all that loved the deceased Queene, and honor the living King." Some interest attaches to Chettle's mention of contemporary poets under pastoral names, including Shakespeare as Melicert. Also indebted to both Sannazaro and Spenser are the *Piscatorie Eclogs* appended to Phineas Fletcher's *The Purple Island* (1633).

There is bucolic masquerade too in *The Shepheards Hunting* (1615) by the wordy and contentious George Wither (1588–1667). This set of five long eclogues reprints two that had appeared in the previous year as an appendix to William Browne of Tavistock's collection *The Shepheards Pipe*: Browne appears as Willy, and Wither himself as Roget; the principal subject of their discourse is Wither's imprisonment in the Marshalsea, and the "shepherd's hunting" of the title is Wither's career as a satirist which had landed him in prison. Wither's *Fair Virtue* (1622) is a shapeless medley of pastoral description and song which extends to nearly five thousand lines. Wither, like Barnfield, is best in short pieces, such as that delightful evocation of the undergraduate's salad days, "I loved a lass a fair one," with its idyllic glimpses of the Oxford countryside.

The greatest pastoralist among Spenser's disciples is Michael Drayton (1563–1631). His pastoral name "Rowland of the Rock" was often linked to Colin Clout's in contemporary complimentary verse, and his first pastorals, a set of nine "eglogs" entitled *Idea, the Shepheards Garland* (1593), betray clearly, in structure, subject, language, and meter, the influence of *The Shepheardes Calender*. Thus the first and last eclogues are love laments by Rowland himself, the seventh is a debate between youth and age, and the third is a panegyric upon Elizabeth, here called "Beta" to complement Spenser's praise of Elisa. The fourth in some ways complements Spenser's *Astrophel*, since its central passage is a lament for a dead shepherd who represents Sidney. The only tune in Spenser's poem that finds no echo in Drayton's is the religious and political satire. Drayton ignores allegories of shepherd as Christian pastor in order to concentrate upon the equation between shepherd and poet. His subject is not man's whole life, of which the twelve months of *The Shepheardes Calender* are emblematic, but the poet's craft, as he indicates in his subtitle, "Rowland's Sacrifice to the nine Muses."

The freshest of the eclogues is the eighth, in which the burlesque tone of a mock-romance reminiscent of Chaucer's "Sir Thopas" is offset by affectionate regionalism; for the setting is Drayton's beloved Warwickshire, and the delicious beauty of Dowsabell, heroine of the tale, is defined by reference to good things of the Midland countryside, such as Leominster wool, the grass that grows beside the Derbyshire Dove, and the swan that swims in the Trent (lines 147–52). Dowsabell loves and is loved by a jolly shepherd, and their happy little wooing dialogue acts as a corrective to Rowland's love complaints in other eclogues. The mood and technique of this poem are close to the pastoral ballads found in contemporary broadsides and miscellanies. While in no sense "realistic," it draws some of its vitality from the wooing games of real country people.

English country games crop up unexpectedly in Drayton's *Endimion and Phoebe: Ideas Latmus* (1595) when satyrs on Mount Latmus play barley-break. This poem is one of those Ovidian mythological narratives so fashionable in the 1590s, of which Marlowe's *Hero and Leander* (written 1590) and Shakespeare's *Venus and Adonis* (1593) are best known; but though Drayton borrows from Marlowe and

Shakespeare, his treatment of love, in accordance with the myth he has chosen, is Platonic and almost entirely without their eroticism. Endimion is, of course, a shepherd, and his home upon the slopes of Mount Latmus has all the features of the Arcadia described by Sannazaro. *Endimion and Phoebe* was considerably cut and extensively revised when it appeared in Drayton's collected *Poems* (1606) under the title of "The Man in the Moone." Here the myth becomes a tale told by old Rowland at a shepherds' feast in honor of Pan, and is linked to this framework by a satirical passage about misdeeds of shepherds as observed by the man in the moon. The satire, the framework, and the identity of the tale-teller all serve to make the poem something of an oversized eclogue, and to link it with Drayton's *Eglogs* which it immediately follows in the 1606 collection.

These *Eglogs* are a complete rewriting and rearrangement of *The Shepheards Garland* with the substitution of a new ninth eclogue. Drayton's revisions introduce a new note of satirical bitterness. For instance, in the sixth eclogue, a rehandling of the fourth in *The Shepheards Garland*, the deaths of Sidney and Queen Elizabeth (and the accession of the "Northerne" monarch, James I) are made to signify the death of an old order of virtue, poetry, and patronage:

> The Groves, the Mountaynes, and the pleasant Heath,
> That wonted were with Roundelayes to ring,
> Are blasted now with the cold Northerne breath,
> That not a Shepheard takes delight to sing.[4] (85–88)

Despite such occasional asperity, the dominant mood of this series, as of the earlier series of eclogues, is delight in the poet's art and in the English landscape. The setting of the ninth eclogue is just such a sheep-shearing feast in the Cotswold Hills as the one described in Drayton's *Poly-Olbion*, song 14, and depicted on the map for that song. The songs in the ninth eclogue are marked by such refined and formalized hyperbole as that[5] which represents Sylvia, the moorland maiden, staying the course of nature and defying mutability:

> *Motto.* Why doth the Sunne against his kind,
>   Stay his bright Chariot in the Skies?
> *Perkin.* He pawseth, almost strooken blind,
>   With gazing on her heavenly Eyes...

Motto. How come those Flowres to flourish still,
        Not withering with sharpe Winters breath?
Perkin. Shee hath rob'd Nature of her skill,
        And comforts all things with her breath.
Motto. Why slide these Brookes so slow away,
        As swift as the wild Roe that were?
Perkin. O, muse not Shepheard, that they stay,
        When they her Heavenly voice doe heare.
                                        (149–52, 157–64)

Thus Perkin expresses the timeless quality of his love as well as the
excellence of his mistress. The exquisite formality of this song satis-
fyingly balances the vivid and sympathetic rustic observation in the
setting.

Balance is lost in *The Shepheards Sirena* published with *The
Battaile of Agincourt* in 1627, but probably written about thirteen
years earlier. The lyric, "Neare to the Silver *Trent, Sirena* dwelleth,"
is one of the finest of its age; the "framework" has shepherds and
shepherdesses who sing roundelays and dance "trenchmore," but they
also fight to prevent swineherds invading the sheep walks with their
hogs and rooting up the pastures. There is an allegory here, which
Drayton leaves obscure (and deliberately so if the "Angry Olcon"
who encourages these swineherds is James I, as most commentators
believe),[6] but the asperity of this passage is out of key with the rest
of the eclogue. This same 1627 volume contains Drayton's exercise
in the fashionable minor Jacobean-Caroline genre of fairy poetry:
Nimphidia, a happy piece of mock-heroic whimsy. Its fairies owe
most to art, but something to a still living rustic superstition too:

        These make our Girles their sluttery rue,
        By pinching them both blacke and blew,
        And put a penny in their shue,
            The house for cleanly sweeping.   (65–68)

Fairy lore and rustic custom find their way together into Drayton's
last pastoral *The Muses Elizium* (1630), the eighth "Nimphall" of
which is a prothalamion celebrating the wedding of a nymph and a
fay. In several nimphalls Elizium is contrasted with the ironically
named Felicia, a once paradisal and now wretched region which
represents the real world, or specifically England;[7] and in the tenth

nimphall Drayton introduces himself, in the character of an aged satyr, fleeing from plague-stricken Felicia and coming to Elizium, that "Paradise on earth," without tempest or winter, where delights never fade, where brooks are decked with lilies, and trees always laden with ripe fruit, where sit "Apolloes prophets," and before them sing the Muses and dance the Graces:

> Decay nor Age there nothing knowes,
> There is continuall Youth,
> As Time on plant or creatures growes,
> So still their strength renewth.
>
> The Poets Paradise this is,
> To which but few can come;
> The Muses only bower of blisse
> Their Deare *Elizium*. (97–104)

This Paradise is the world of literary art itself, and *The Muses Elizium* as a whole represents Drayton's furthest development in pastoral toward pure aesthetic patterning and the creation of pleasing forms that are freed from any reference to objective reality.

An alternative development of pastoral toward idyllic loco-descriptive poetry may be observed *in extenso* in Drayton's *Poly-Olbion* (part 1, 1612; part 2, 1622), a thirty-thousand-line-long poetical guide book to the rivers, mountains, forests, antiquities, legend, customs, natural resources, and occupations of all the counties of England and Wales. Drayton's address "to the Generall *Reader*" promises him a journey through "delicate embrodered Meadowes, often veined with gentle gliding Brooks; in which thou maist fully view the dainty Nymphes in their simple naked bewties, bathing them in Crystalline streames; which shall lead thee, to most pleasant Downes, where harmlesse Shepheards are, some exercising their pipes, some singing roundelaies, to their gazing flocks"; and the maps that preface each of the thirty songs show a nymph in every stream and a shepherd on every hill. In order to dramatize his catalog of the varied beauties of the English countryside he uses the machinery of classical pastoral, the local deities; thus the nymph of the Irwell boasts of that river's beauty and incidentally paints a familiar picture of the well-being and gaiety of English country folk:

Yee lustie Lasses then, in *Lancashire* that dwell,
For Beautie that are sayd to beare away the Bell,
Your countries Horn-pipe, ye so minsingly that tread,
As ye the Eg-pye love, and Apple Cherry-red;
In all your mirthfull Songs, and merry meetings tell,
That *Erwell* every way doth *Ribble* farre excell.   (65–70)

Allegorical satire in *The Shepheards Sirena* directed against those
unidentified bad poets who defile beautiful and sacred old sheep-
walks reappears in Drayton's commendatory verses "to his friend
the Author" which preface *Britannia's Pastorals, Book I* by William
Browne (1690–45?). Drayton welcomes this young pastor to the
company of true shepherds who continue the Spenserian tradition;
but Browne, like Drayton, diverges further from Spenser the more he
writes. *Britannia's Pastorals* (book 1, 1613; book 2, 1616; and a
fragment of book 3 written in the 1620s) is a discursive narrative
poem founded upon hints from Ovid, Sannazaro, Tasso, Sidney, *The
Faerie Queene*, and John Fletcher's pastoral play *The Faithful Shepherdess*. Browne's romantic action finds a place for a varied cast of
shepherds and shepherdesses, Olympian Gods, lustful satyrs, Grecian
local deities, Devonshire fairies and personifications of Truth, Time,
and Riot. Though it is the longest narrative pastoral poem in the
language it is technically a series of eclogues because it consists of a
succession of songs which are sung by a shepherd to an audience of
fellow shepherds. At the end of each song the narrative is broken
off, as night falls, or as rain begins, or as a sheep caught in a brake
requires the singer's attention. Browne follows the Elizabethan poets'
fashion of localizing classical myth, and transporting a whole system
of pagan deities, nymphs, and satyrs to the England of their own day:
indeed, his true subject is the English countryside and its people. He
asks at the opening of book 1, song 1:

What need I tune the Swaines of *Thessaly?*
Or, bootlesses, adde to them of *Arcadie?* . . .
My *Muse* for lofty pitches shall not rome
And homely pipen of her native home   (9–10, 13–14)[8]

and the complicated romantic action is often relieved by glimpses of
the people of Browne's native home, Devonshire, at work in the fields

or at play at a May game or rustic wedding. A characteristic passage
is the following from book 2, song 1:

> Long on the shore distrest *Marina* lay:
> For he that ope's the pleasant sweets of *May*,
> Beyond the *Noonstead* so farre drove his teame,
> That harvest folkes, with curds and clouted creame,
> With cheese and butter, cakes, and oates ynow,
> That are the *Yeomans*, from the yoke or Cowe,
> On sheaves of corne were at their noonshuns close,
> Whilst by them merrily the *Bagpipe* goes:
> Ere from her hand she lifted up her head,
> Where all the *Graces* then inhabited.
> When casting round her over-drowned eyes,
> (So have I seen a Gemme of mickle price
> Roll in a Scallop-shell with water fild)
> She, on a marble rocke at hand behild,
> In Characters deepe cut with Iron stroke,
> A Shepheards moane, which, read by her, thus spoke:
> > Glide soft, ye silver Floods,
> >   And every Spring:
> > Within the shady Woods
> >   Let no Bird sing!
> Nor from the Grove a *Turtle-Dove*
> Be seene to couple with her love:
> But silence on each Dale and Mountaine dwell,
> Whilst *Willy* bids his friend and joy *Farewell*.   (225–48)

Heroic action is suspended for a moment as Browne gives the time of
day with a reference to harvesters, before he continues, by way of
the pearl conceit, to the higher style of his stately lyric. These Devonshire vignettes, or idylls (if we retain the meaning of eidullion, "a
little picture"), often appear in the form of extended similes, such
as the angler and the squirrel-hunt in book 1, song 5. Such characteristic thumbnail sketches as "A Little Lad set on a banke to
shale / The ripened Nuts" (book 2, song 4) have an immediacy and
clarity that contrast strikingly with the overall narrative.

The local patriotism that underlies the whole work is proudly
declared in book 2, song 3: "Haile, thou my native soile! thou
blessed plot / Whose equal all the world affordeth not!" (602–3).
Such patriotism is given a specifically pastoral character in book 2,

song 4, where an aged shepherd is drawn from his story of Pan and
Syrinx into a digression that is unusually distant even for Browne:

> And now, ye Brittish Swains (Whose harmlesse sheepe
> Then all the worlds beside I joy to keepe,
> Which spread on every Plaine and hilly Wold
> Fleeces no lesse esteem'd then that of gold,
> For whose exchange one *Indy Iems* of price,
> The other gives you of her choicest spice.   (933–38)

Britain's exports of wool and woollen goods were to become a well-
loved and well-worn theme for the patriotic poets of the following
century, but those poets would regard with less equanimity than
Browne the foreign luxuries for which wool was exchanged. An
anticipation of another favorite eighteenth-century theme occurs when,
in book 2, song 3, Browne assures his readers that golden-age shepherds are blessed with natural reason:

> O happy men! you ever did possesse
> No wisedome but was mixt with simplenesse;
> So wanting malice and from folly free,
> Since reason went with your simplicite.   (426–29)

Drayton, Wither, and Browne presented themselves as a group—
using pastoral often to celebrate the friendships of poets. In their
work there was a tendency to "naturalize" the pastoral to the English
scene; they viewed Elizabethan England retrospectively as a golden
age. As late as the 1620s, in an age when poetic fashions inclined
either toward "strong lines" or Horatian urbanity, they took Spenser
as their model. However, it is the more relaxed, even homely, elements in Spenser that they inherited; the symbolism of *The Shepheardes Calender* was beyond them. Thus beside their master they
appear comparatively unserious.

Chapter Six

Elizabethan and Jacobean Pastoral Lyric

Apart from the elaborate constructs of Browne and Drayton and other writers of formal eclogue there is a huge quantity of Elizabethan and Jacobean pastoral lyrical verse. Pastoral song was the common property of court, city, and country. Among the popular broadside ballads sung and sold by itinerant ballad-singers are many fine pastorals which testify to the fact that the period from the accession of Elizabeth to the outbreak of the Civil War was the golden age of popular song. The many Elizabethan, Jacobean, and Caroline collections of madrigals and lute songs, which appear to have been bought mostly by the middle classes, give a prominent place to pastorals. Few royal entertainments for Elizabeth or James or Charles were complete without a pastoral song. Pastoral lyrics appear of course in pastoral stage plays and prose romances, but they are inserted often into plays and prose narrative that are not predominantly pastoral in character.

Some work of a pastoral kind is to be found in all of the Elizabethan poetical miscellanies from the most courtly, *The Phoenix Nest* (1593), to the most popular, *A Handfull of Pleasant Delights* (1566, 1576, 1584), which latter consists entirely of reprints of broadside ballads; but a modern reader can most conveniently assess the quality and variety of all but the most humble types by reading *England's Helicon* (1600; enlarged 1614),[1] which is unique among the miscellanies in that it contains nothing but pastorals. Its editor was Nicholas Ling who for the most part took printed poems and revised them freely, sometimes changing titles or speakers, or even introducing new verses in order to ensure that all conformed to the pastoral character of the whole anthology.

The theme of nearly all the great chorus of pastoral song from the court to the street is love in all its moods, from the idealization of a cruelly chaste mistress, to a healthy joy in sexual fruition, or to plain bawdry. The first is more characteristic of academic and courtly pastoral and the last of the popular type, but the division between courtly and popular is not hard and fast, and many of the great successes of Elizabethan-Jacobean pastoral lyric occur where courtly-classical and Renaissance-Italian elements are united with a native popular tradition of song and ballad.

There are few exact English equivalents to the medieval French "pastourelle"[2] which tells how a young courtier rides out on a spring morning, meets a lovely shepherdess, listens to her singing, abruptly offers his love (sometimes with the promises of fine robes or jewels), overcomes her refusals, and enjoys her. In English handling of this material the suiter usually is outwitted; a typical example is the ballad of "The Baffled Knight" which was printed in Thomas Raven-croft's *Deuteromelia* (1609) and appeared subsequently in many other versions.[3] There are traces of pastourelle in the rustic wooing-dialogues associated with jigs and mimes performed on holiday occasions by English country folk.[4] A late medieval example of the wooing dialogue still well-known in Elizabethan times began: " 'hey, troly loly lo, maid, whither go you?' / 'I go to the meadow to milk my cow.' " On that occasion the lover does not persuade the milkmaid to yield; but he woos to better success in another song of the same period, "Come over the woodes faire and green, / Thou goodly maid, thou lusty wench," and contrives to pick "that fair flower that ye have kept so long."[5] The finest of these late medieval pastoral wooing-dialogues is "Robene and Makyne" by Robert Henryson (1430?–1506).

Among popular broadside pastoral ballads, one of the largest groups consists of lighthearted and circumstantial descriptions of seductions in idyllic surroundings. There is no need to assume that these derive from the pastourelle or the pseudo-Theocritean idyll 27. The subject matter is common enough in such typical pieces as "A Merry New Ballad of a Country Wench and a Clown"[6] among the Shirburn Ballads, or "The Coy Shepherdess"[7] in the Roxburghe Collection:

> *Phillis* on the new made hay
> On a pleasant Summers day
> She in wanton posture lay
> thinking no shephard nigh her.

A respectable counterpart to such ballads is found in Nicholas Breton's three-part song "Phillida and Corydon" in *The Entertainment given to the Queen at Elvetham* (1591), reprinted in *England's Helicon*. Other large groups of popular ballads are complaints of seduced, abandoned shepherdesses, and of shepherds whose love is unrequited. Among the first the old "As I rode out" formula of the pastourelle frequently survives as, for example, in the early seventeenth-century ballad "The Broom of Cowdenowes." Lovelorn shepherds commonly wear a willow garland, such as the one alluded to in Desdemona's song. A celebrated ballad, "The Shepheards Lamentation" (1613) — "Come Shepheards decke your heads no more with bayes but willows" — is one of the songs mentioned by Izaac Walton's milkwoman in *The Compleat Angler*.

A more elaborate courtly counterpart of this kind of ballad may be found in "Harpalus Complaynt." This poem appeared in *Tottle's Miscellany* (1557; nine more editions to 1587) and, with variants, in *England's Helicon* (where it was attributed, probably mistakenly, to the earl of Surrey); it was registered, too, as a broadside ballad in 1564–65, and thus like other poems from the miscellanies enjoyed a popular circulation. Harpalus has been rejected, so he heaps his anathemas upon cruel Phillida and forecasts his own death, in token of which he wears a mourning willow wreath; and, as pastoral life should be close to Nature, he indicates the unnaturalness of Phillida's behavior by reference to birds and beasts around them:

> The Hart he feedeth by the Hind,
> the Bucke hard by the Doe:
> The Turtle-Dove is not unkind
> to him that loves her so.
> The Ewe she hath by the Ram,
> the young Cowe hath the Bull. (69–74)

Phillida's behavior is unnatural; external Nature pursues its course indifferent to the affairs of shepherds: by contrast in "The Unknown

Sheepheards Complaint," Nature is overset by the lover's sorrow
resulting from his mistress's coldness:

> Clear Wells spring not, sweet birds sing not,
> Greene plants bring not foorth their die:
> Heards stand weeping, Flocks all sleeping,
> Nimphs back peeping fearefully.

This wholehearted lyrical exercise in the pathetic fallacy appeared in
Weelkes's *Madrigals* (1597), *The Passionate Pilgrim* (1599), and, of
course, *England's Helicon*, where it was followed by "Another of
same Sheepheards," which consists of a long extract from Barnfield's
song "As it fell upon a day / In the merry moneth of May," omitting the nonpastoral part and adding a new terminal couplet. In this
lyric the lover compares his own sorrows to those of the unhappy
legendary nightingale Philomela. The lyric which follows next in
England's Helicon is from Thomas Watson's *Hekatompathia* (1582),
and in it the sorrowful shepherd compares "his owne amorous in-
felicitie to the offence of Actaeon." This is followed next by a lyric
from Thomas Lodge's *Rosalynde* (1590), "Montanus Sonnet to his
faire *Phoebe*," where the lover likens himself to the "love-sicke
Polipheme." So the complaints with their mythical parallels continue
throughout *England's Helicon*. "The sheepheard Eurymachus to his
faire sheepheardesse *Mirimida*," reprinted from Robert Green's *Fran-
cesco's Fortunes* (1590), uses the conventional figures of mythology
in sketching the bright landscape that contrasts with the lover's sorrow:

> When *Flora* proud in pompe of all her flowers
>   sat bright and gay:
> And gloried in the dewe of *Iris* showers,
>   and did display
> Her mantle checquer'd all with gaudie greene,
>   Then I
>   alone
> A mournfull man in *Ericine* was seene.

The main purpose of the poem however is to explore a conceit that
likens lovers to salamanders because they

> live within the fire
> Of fervent love:

> And shrinke not from the flame of hote desire,
> Nor will not move
> From any heate that *Venus* force imparts:
> But lie
> content,
> Within a fire, and waste away their harts.

Greene's speaker is a shepherd, but his song has little reference to pastoral life, actual or imagined. Though love-complaints bulk largest, *England's Helicon* includes songs celebrating a happy and uncomplicated fulfillment in love—for shepherds such as Henry Constable's Damelus who sings to his

> *Diaphenia* like the Daffedown-dillie,
> White as the Sunne, faire as the Lillie
> heigh hoe, how I doo love thee—

and for shepherdesses such as Lodge's Rosalynde who sings her sugary little Madrigal:

> Love in my bosome like a Bee,
> dooth suck his sweete:
> Now with his wings he playes with me,
> now with his feete.

In "*Coridons* Song," also reprinted in *England's Helicon* from Lodge's *Rosalynde*, a blithe and bonny country lass who wants a husband is successfully wooed by a "smicker Boy, a lither Swaine." So, too, in Nicholas Breton's "Phillida and Coridon" Phillida's pretended reluctance is soon overcome.

The course of love is more interestingly complicated in Breton's "*Astrophell* his Song of *Phillida* and *Coridon*" (*England's Helicon*), where the conventional courtly love situation of the lover adoring his mistress as the luminary of his life and the bestower of grace and virtue is linked with a social relationship; for the beloved is the shepherd's employer:

> Poore *Coridon* dooth keepe the fields,
> though *Phillida* be she that owes them:
> And *Phillida* dooth walke the Meades,
> though *Coridon* be he that mowes them.

> The little Lambs are *Phillis* love,
>> though *Coridon* is he that feedes them:
> The Gardens faire are *Phillis* ground,
>> though *Coridon* be he that weedes them
> Since then that *Phillis* onely is,
>> the onely Sheepheards onely Queene:
> And *Coridon* the onely Swaine,
>> that onely hath her Sheepheard beene.
> Though *Phillis* keepe her bower of state,
>> shall *Coridon* consume away:
> No Sheepheard no, worke out the weeke,
> And Sunday shall be holy-day.

Breton, like so many other pastoralists of his generation, brings the gracefulness of the ideal world of conventional pastoral into the workday English countryside in order to show how man's hopes and aspirations can healthfully transcend the limitations of humdrum life. His "Shall we go daunce the hay" (*England's Helicon*) ends "the sport was scarce begun: but I wakt, and all was done." It is noteworthy that three of his eight pastoral poems in *England's Helicon* are cast in the form of dreams.

If Breton's success lies in the reservations that he implies when he places the pastoral dream within ordinary life, the triumphs of Marlowe's "The Passionate Sheepheard to his love" ("Come live with me and be my love"), and the "Reply" attributed to Ralegh lie in their singleheartedness in fully embracing or absolutely denying that dream of an ideal timeless Arcadian world. Four stanzas of the first and one of the second had been printed in *The Passionate Pilgrim* (1599). The two songs in their *England's Helicon* versions were united to form a single broadside ballad, and were sung responsively by the milkmaid and her mother in *The Compleat Angler*. Ralegh's reply, by introducing the concept of time, "The flowers doe fade, and wanton fieldes, / To wayward winter reckoning yeeldes," contradicts Marlowe's golden-age image of a perpetual May-time, and thus denies Marlowe's implication that love is unchanging. Marlowe's was one of the best known, most imitated, and most parodied of all Elizabethan poems.[8] An anonymous imitation follows Ralegh's "Reply" in *England's Helicon*; Donne wrote a piscatory imitation, "The Baite," which was reprinted in *The Compleat Angler*; Herrick wrote an imitation (see chap. 7), and Charles Cotton wrote two. Breton has a devotional version, "Emmanuell": "Come live with mee, and be my love, / My love, my life, my King my god."[9] By contrast *The Westminister Drolleries* (1671) includes a popular ballad parody beginning "Come live with me and be my whore."[10] Less earthy, but still relatively mundane, is the dialect piece "A wooeing Song of a Yeoman of Kent's son" in Thomas Ravencroft's song book *Melismata* (1611) where the wooer promises the solid advantages of his house and land in Kent, his hog, and his sow. Among the invitations to love in *England's Helicon*, one at last can stand comparison with Marlowe's. This is an anonymous *aubade* taken from John Dowland's *First Booke of Songes or Ayres* (1597) which begins:

> Come away, come sweet Love,
> The golden morning Breakes:
> All the earth, all the ayre,
> Of love and pleasure speakes.

Here loves' urgency is felt:

> Come away, come sweet Love,
> The golden morning wasts . . .
> sweet Love let us hie
> Flying, dying in desire:
> Wing'd with sweet hopes and heavenly fire.

This is the spirit of *carpe diem*. The "golden morning" implies a dusky evening; it is not the timeless golden world that is implied in Marlowe's invitation.

The classical notion of the Golden Age, particularly in its Ovidian form, appears frequently in Elizabethan pastoral, but it appears also in the newer shape of a libertine paradise of free love. It is celebrated as such in Samuel Daniel's "A Pastorall" (*Works*, 1601) which is a translation of a chorus in act 1 of Tasso's pastoral play *Aminta* (acted 1573). In this chorus Tasso elaborates a hint in Tibullus, *Elegies* II, and claims that the first age was golden not because the earth enjoyed eternal springtime, not because rivers ran with streams of milk and honey dropped from trees, not because warfare and trading were unknown, but because "the tyrant of the mind," Honor, had not yet assumed his sway:

Nor were his hard lawes knowne to free-borne hearts.
But golden lawes like these.
Which nature wrote. *That's lawfull which doth please*...
The naked virgin then,
Her Roses fresh reveales,
Which now her vaile conceales:
The tender Apples in her bosome seene.
And oft in Rivers cleere
The Lovers with their Loves consorting were.[11]

Such a pastoral acts out the desire to escape from moral responsibility
into a world where free and easy love enlivens rather than disturbs
otium. This is far from the world of Colin Clout. Significantly, the
Puritan Spenser is at particular pains to reject Tasso's opinion that the
Golden Age was one of libertinism (*Faerie Queene*, bk. 4, canto 8,
stanza 30):

> But antique age yet in the infancie
>   Of time, did live then like an innocent,
>   In simple truth and blamelesse chastitie,
>   Ne then of guile had made experiment,
>   But voide of vile and treacherous intent,
>   Held vertue for itselfe in soveraine awe:
>   Then loyall love had royall regiment,
>   And each unto his lust did make a lawe,
> From all forbidden things his liking to withdraw.

But the view of Tasso and of Daniel regarding the Golden Age is the
one that prevails in the seventeenth century.

Chapter Seven

Merry England and her Enemies

The seasons in the Elizabethan countryside were marked by traditional rituals which still carried traces of pagan nature-worship; popular song grew around these festivals, particularly around the May Day games, and such song duly influenced more learned and courtly poetry. As always in this period, the division between aristocratic, middle-class, and popular literature is not firm. Among popular broadsides are may-pole songs of the "Come lasses and lads" variety: in books of madrigals are such pieces as Thomas Morley's "About the maypole now, with glee" (*First Booke of Balletts to Five Voyces,* 1595), in which Thyrsis and Cloris dance with other shepherds and nymphs: *England's Helicon* includes a song probably by Thomas Watson, "The Nimphes meeting their May Queene," which was sung at the royal entertainment at Elvetham on May Day 1591, where the May queen was Elizabeth herself. Sidney's pastoral entertainment *The Lady of May* (performed 1578 or 1579), employs the shepherds of classical idyll to offer tributes to the queen as England's loveliest May lady; and *The Triumphs of Oriana* (1601),[1] the famous madrigal anthology compiled by Thomas Morley, probably was composed for a royal May-Day pastoral entertainment. The queen loved to dance on May Day and would go Maying with her subjects.

Dancing, May games, and other old rustic customs were under attack however. Philip Stubbes wrote in *The Anatomie of Abuses* (1583):

But the chiefest jewel they bring from thence is their Maypole, which they bring home with great veneration, as thus. They have twentie or

fortie yoke of Oxen, every Oxe having a sweet nosegay of flouers placed
on the tip of his hornes; and these Oxen drawe home this May-pole
(this stinking Ydol, rather) which is covered all over with floures and
hearbs, bound around about with strings from the top to the bottome,
and sometime painted with variable colours, with two or three hundred
men, women and children, following it with great devotion. And thus
beeing reared up with handkercheefs and flags hovering on the top,
they straw the ground round about, binde green boughes about it, set
up summer haules, bowers, and arbors hard by it; and then they fall
to daunce about it like as the heathen people did at the dedication of
the Idols, whereof this is a perfect pattern, or rather the thing itself.

William Prynne followed suit in *Histriomastix* (1633), attacking
dancing, "ridiculous love-pranks," and "amorous Pastorals, or obscene
lascivious love-songs." Puritan magistrates sought to discourage dancing and traditional rural sports and to suppress games of every kind
on Sunday, but James I issued a declaration in 1618 listing lawful
sports. These included "dancing, either men or women; archery for
men; leaping, vaulting, or any other such harmless recreation; May-
games, Whitsun-ales, Morris-dances, and the setting up of Maypoles,
and other sports therewith used, so as the same be had in due and
convenient time, without impediment or neglect of divine service."
Charles I made a similar proclamation in 1633.

The Stuart court continued Elizabeth's patronage of folk-sports and
dancing; and its association with the annual Cotswold Games is celebrated in a little volume, *Annalia Dubrensia*[2] (1636), in which
Jonson, Drayton, Thomas Randolph, Owen Felltham, Thomas Hey-
wood, Shackerly Marmion, and others honored Robert Dover who had
for many years been the organizer of the games and their protector
against the Puritans. Drayton hails Dover as the man "That dost in
these dull iron Times revive / The golden Ages glories." Thomas
Randolph (1605–35) connects the games with pagan antiquity in
"An eclogue on the Palilia and Noble Assemblies revived on Cotswold Hills by Mr. Robert Dover" (the "Palilia" was an ancient
Roman festival in honor of Pales, goddess of sheepfolds and pastures).
Collen complains that, although "*English* pastures, be / As flowery
as the Lawnes of Arcadye" (9–10), English shepherds are dull and
lethargic compared with those of antiquity, because "with their sports,
their soules were tan away":

> Till then they all were active; every day
> They exercis'd to weild their limbes, that now
> Are numb'd to everything, but flaile, and Plowe.
> Early in *May* up got the Jolly route,
> Cal'd by the Larke, and spread the fields aboute:
> One, for to breath himselfe, would coursing bee
> From this same Beech, to yonder Mulberie;
> A second leapt, his supple nerves to trie,
> A third, was practicing his Melodie;
> This, a new Jigg was footing; Others, were
> Busied at wrestling, or to throw the Barre;
> Ambitious which should beare the bell away,
> And kisse the Nut-browne-Lady of the Maie.   (24–36)

They have been deprived of their sports by the Puritans, those "melancholy Swaines" who

> teach that Dauncing is a *Jezabell*,
> And Barley-breake, the ready way to Hell,
> The Morrice, *Idolls*, Whitson-ales can bee
> But profane Reliques, of a *Jubilee*:
> These in a Zeale, t'expresse how much they doe
> The organs hate, have silenc'd Bagg-pipes too,
> And harmlesse May-poles, all are rail'd upon,
> As if they were the Towers of *Babilon*.   (53–60)

But Pan (Charles I) has declared that henceforth dancing shall be holy, and "Joviall Dover" has restored the ancient games that "give the old mirth, and Innocence a new life." The bucolic masks for the king and the Puritans are in context quite appropriate, and the subject matter is genuinely pastoral in this delightful and too little known eclogue.

The struggle between Cavalier and Puritan over this rustic and recreational battlefield did not go unnoticed by poets. Richard Corbett (1583–1635), bishop successively of Oxford and Norwich, makes several allusions to the subject in his light occasional verse. Corbett satirizes a Puritan minister in an ironic "Exhortation to Mr. John Hammon, minister in the parish of Bewdly, for the battering downe of the Vanityes of the Gentiles, which are comprehended in a May-pole; written by a Zealous Brother from the Black-fryers," while in his best-known poem, "The Faeryes Farewell," written, like the "Exhortation," in James I's reign, Corbett gaily associates the Puritans' attack upon old dances and old rustic beliefs with the banishment of Roman Catholic fairies at the Reformation. The anonymous author of *Pasquil's Palinodia* (1634), deploring their overthrow by "peevish puritans," associates May-poles with the sanctities of an ideal social order in the countryside:

> Happy the age and harmlesse were the dayes,
> (For then true love and amity was found,)
> When every village did a May Pole raise,
> And Whitson-ales and May-games did abound:
> And all the lusty yonkers, in a rout,
> With merry lasses daunc'd the rod about,
> Then Friendship to their banquets bid the guests,
> And poore men far'd the better for their feasts.
> The lords of castles, manors, townes, and towers,
> Rejoic'd when they beheld the farmers flourish,
> And would come down unto the summer-bowers
> To see the country-gallants dance the Morrice.[3]

The "good old days" of the recent past could be seen as a blend of good housekeeping and May-pole dancing in poems without such a partisan political edge too. A full picture of an English rustic golden age, the "Merry England" of Elizabeth's heyday, is offered by Nicholas Breton in "Mad-caps oh the merrie time"[4] (1602). He asks "Oh where is now that goodly *golden time?*" "When *Nymphes* and *Muses* sweetly kept the woods, / And olde Hob-goblin kept within the caves" (64–65). The old England was a place for curds and cream and hearty good living for rich and poor alike, when

> every Farmer kept good household fare,
> And not a rich man would a beggar rate
> But he would give him almes at his gate.   (26–28)

It was an age of truth, innocence and honesty, before Machiavellianism and coney-catching were known. Food was cheap—"one might have a hundred *eggs a groate*"—and love was free—on May mornings "*Batchelors* gave wenches a greene gowne" (152). Plain dealing and simple traditional amusements went together:

The *Farmer* sought not for his neighbours goods.
But *Sam* and *Simkin* were the merry slaves,
That danced *Trenchmore* on their grandsirs graves.   (66–68)

... Pipe and Tabor made as merry glee
As at a May-pole one would wish to see.   (160–61)

Breton's lighthearted amalgam of Nymphs, Muses, Hobgoblins, May-poles, dancing farm servants, generous farmers, and the rest demonstrates the ease with which early seventeenth-century poets could "naturalize" the classical pastoral not only to the English landscape, as the earlier Elizabethans had done, but to the social relationships of English rural life.

Shackerly Marmion in his contribution to *Annalia Dubrensia* bestows the usual praise upon Dover for reviving the worship of Pan and transforming the Cotswolds into Arcadia; but, interestingly, the bogy who threatens the Arcadian joys of English shepherds is not the censorious Puritan, but the sordid, commercially minded enclosing monopolistic landowner.

Even in the idyllic world of Browne's *Britannia's Pastorals* there are complaints about the engrossing of farms (that is, the buying out of poor neighbours and eviction of tenants-at-will on small-holdings in order to create huge "economically viable" units, which were commonly turned over to sheep-farming):

> The *Country-Gentleman*, from Neighbour's hand,
> Forceth th' Inheritance, joins Land to Land;
> And (most insatiate) seeks under his Rent,
> To bring the World's most spacious Continent
> (bk. 2, song 1, ll. 871–74)

and the engrossing and regrating of corn (that is, keeping it from the market and creating an artificial scarcity to push up prices): "The griping *Farmer* hoards the Seed of Bread, / Whilst, in the Street, the Poore lye famished" (879–80). Browne, however, offers his readers at last the improbable assurance that the shepherd is uniquely happy: "And free, there's none, from all this worldly strife, / Except the Shepherd's Heaven-blest happy Life" (881–82).

The first collection of formal verse satire in English, Joseph Hall's *Virgidemiarum* (1597, 1598), includes in book 5 complaints about rack-renting, engrossing, and enclosure (satires 1 and 3), and about the decay of "housekeeping" by great landowners (satire 2, which probably gave hints for Pope's portrait of Cotta in the *Epistle to Bathurst*). Such complaints are a recurrent theme in sermons, stage plays, and popular ballads of the sixteenth and seventeenth centuries. A particular source of social protest lay in what might be described as the mercenary pastoralism of great landowners who, seeing where the profits of husbandry lay, bought up or evicted their poorer neighbors and enclosed common land to create huge sheep farms which were much less "labour intensive" than arable holdings; so that whole villages disappeared, nothing but a shepherd's hut remaining.[5] In *Virgidemiarum*, book 5, satire 1, Hall alludes to this practice and claims that dispossessed small farmers are being driven overseas. He refers to the avaricious landlord who would

> dislodge whole Collonies of poore,
> And lay their roofe quite levell with their floore...
> And ships them to the new-nam'd Virgin-land,
> Or wilder wales, where never wight yet wond:

and addresses the evicted tenant: "Would it not vexe thee where thy syres did keepe, / To see the dunged foldes of dag-tayled sheepe?"[6] (99–100, 113–16). Incidentally, the poor tenant's hereditary home has earlier been described with a sleazy particularity that rivals Virgil's *Moretum*:

> Of one bayes breadth, God wot, a silly cote,
> Whose thatched Spars are furr'd with sluttish soote
> A whole inch thick, shining like Black-moors browns
> Through smoke that down the head-les barrel blows.
> At his beds-feete feeden his stalled teme,
> His swine beneath, his pullen ore the beame.   (59–64)

Hall's sermons similarly denounce "the oppressing gentleman, who tyrannizes over his cottagers, encroaches upon his neighbour's inheritance, encloses commons, depopulates villages, and screws his tenants to death."[7] Denunciations by Latimer, Tyndale, and other earlier Tudor preachers against enclosures for large-scale sheep farming are echoed in popular verse. The aphorism in More's *Utopia* concerning "man-eating sheep" is repeated in a ballad by Richard Cox (1499–

1581), "The Black Shepe,"[8] which tells of six hundred houses now turned into molehills and half England nought but sheep, for the black sheep swallows all. An anonymous ballad, "Christmas's Lamentation," written between 1590 and 1615, neatly unites several common themes of rural complaint with the mythology of literary pastoral, while invoking, in its reference to Piers Plowman, an old native tradition of satire in which the humble countryman is a moral norm:

> Houses where pleasure once did abound,
> Nought but a dog and a shepherd is found,
> Welladay!
> Places where Christmas revels did keep,
> Now are become habitations for sheep. . . .
>
> Pan, the shepherd's god, doth deface,
> Doth deface Lady Ceres' Crown,
> And the tillage doth go to decay,
> To decay in every town;
> Landlord their rents so highly enhance,
> That Pierce, the Ploughman, barefoot may dance;
> Welladay!
> Farmers, that Christmas would still entertain,
> Scarce have wherewith themselves to maintain.[9]

The ideal social relationships in the countryside whose breach is deplored in such satires are represented most memorably in Jonson's "To Penhurst" in *The Forrest* (1616). The original for Jonson's poem is a long epigram by Martial (A.D. 42?–102), which contrasts the flashy, unproductive suburban estate of Bassus with the more modest but useful property of Faustinus at Baiae. Martial describes the cheerful, busy activity of Faustinus's household, the simple gifts brought by visiting neighbors, and the generous hospitality of the owner of the house. Similarly Jonson shows Penshurst, once the home of Sir Philip Sidney, as the center of a healthful tight-knit community living virtuously under the genial influence of a benevolent landlord. Jonson's statement of the social virtues of "housekeeping" is not without some traces of pastoral idyll, for Pan and Bacchus make their feasts beneath the beech and chestnut trees at Penshurst. In "To Sir Robert Wroth" Jonson similarly naturalizes Saturn's reign and the mythical world of pastoral to an English country estate in the course of a verse epistle that owes most to Horace and to Virgil's *Georgics*, book 2.

These works by Jonson stand in a line running from Barclay's fourth eclogue (see chap. 3) of poems idealizing social relations on a country estate.[10] Such works are idyllic in conception and borrow much from the regular pastoral eclogue tradition. Thus Sir Richard Fanshawe (1608–66) sees "White Peace," banished from Saturn's realm when Jove usurped the throne, dwelling now in the English countryside. This is in his "Ode, upon occasion of His Majesties Proclamation in the Year 1630, commanding the Gentry to reside upon their Estates in the Countrey," and the occasion reminds us that Charles I's attempted defense of rural sanctities extended to "housekeeping" as well as to such things as May games. Another courtier poet, Lucius Carey, Lord Falkland (1610–43), paints the joys of country retirement and echoes the philosophic passages of the conclusion to Virgil's *Georgics*, book 2, in a formal funeral eclogue, "Eclogue on the Death of Ben Jonson."

That melodious court poet Thomas Carew (1594–1640) wrote two country house poems closely imitative of Jonson—"To Saxham" and "To my Friend G. N. from Wrest" (*Poems*, 1640), but more characteristically he turns social relationships in the countryside to the service of a persuasion to love when, in his most famous poem "A Rapture," he insolently declares that "Honour" is a term coined "By greedy men, that seeke to enclose the common, / And within private armes empale free woman."[11] Carew's starting points are the pseudo-Theocritean idyll 27 and the first chorus in act 1 of Tasso's *Aminta*, but his poem is far more expansively licentious than either of those. Richard Lovelace (1618–57?) follows Tasso, with less circumstantial sensuality but no less gusto than Carew, in "Love made in the First Age: To Chloris," in *Lucasta* (1649):

> Thrice happy was that Golden Age,...
> When cursed No stain'd no Maids Blisse...
> Lasses like *Autumne* Plums did drop,
> And Lads, indifferently did crop
> A Flower, and a Maiden-head.[12]

Both Carew and Lovelace wrote erotic "Pastoral Dialogues" in which a shepherd and nymph make love in the presence of a chorus or another shepherd, giving the effect of a pastoral peepshow.

The amatory verse of Robert Herrick (1591–1674) is unusually prurient even for its period, but in his poems of English country life he more happily distils a healthy spirit of classical paganism than, perhaps, any other English poet. In one of the introductory poems to *Hesperides* (1648, but containing many poems written in the 1620s) Herrick writes of his "Eclogues" and "Beucolicks," but only a few of his poems are formal eclogues. He has an affable complimentary "Eclogue, or Pastorall between Endimion Porter and Lycidas Herrick, set and sung," a burlesque "Bucolick betwixt Two: Lacon and Thyrsis," and courtly panegyrics in "A Pastorall sung to the King" and "A Pastorall upon the Birth of Prince Charles," both of which were set to music. "The Cruell Maid" is based upon the pseudo-Theocritean idyll 23, though Herrick, like other imitators of this idyll, changes the sex of the beloved.

Much more spirited than any of these is Herrick's exercise in the Passionate Shepherd to his Love vein, "To Phillis, to love, and live with him." He offers an alluring range of rural dainties, including "The Paste of Filberts for thy bread / With Cream of Cowslips buttered,"[13] promises that Phillis will preside over the Shearing Feasts and annual wakes, i.e., church patronal festivals, and rises to gay fooling as he elaborates upon the conventional "blushing" apple:

> In wicker-baskets Maids shall bring
> To thee, (my dearest Shephardling)
> The Blushing Apple, bashfull Peare,
> And shame-fac't Plum, (all simp'ring there).

"To Phillis" is much closer than the formal eclogues to those central concerns of his secular verse set out by Herrick in "The Argument of his Book":

> I sing of *Brooks*, of *Blossoms, Birds*, and *Bowers*:
> Of *April, May*, of *June*, and *July*-Flowers
> I sing of *May-poles, Hock-carts*,[14] *Wassails, Wakes*,
> Of *Bride-grooms, Brides*, and of their *Bridall-cakes*.
> I write of *Youth*, of *Love*, and have Accesse
> By these, to sing of cleanly-*Wantonesse*.

Herrick's most memorable pastoral verse celebrates those festivals of
the country-folk which are tied to the cycle of the seasons, while
"cleanly-wantonness" sums up what the pastoral balladists of the
previous age had desiderated in court and city ladies but found in
the country wench.

Herrick's country-festival verses, naturally enough, usually take the
form of invitations. In "The Wake" he calls,

> Come *Anthea* let us two
> Go to Feast, as others do.
> Tarts and Custards, Creams and Cakes,
> Are the Junketts still at Wakes . . .

and invites his mistress to patronize with him the Robin Hood games,
the Morris dances and the cudgel-play of the "incurious" villagers:
"Happy Rusticks, best content / With the cheapest Merriment." In
"The Hock-cart, or Harvest home" he addresses the harvesters, "Come
Sons of Summer," in order to invite them to the harvest provided
by the lord of the manor and to remind them of their duties to him.
The most famous of these invitations to rustic jollification is also a
gay and pressing invitation to love. This is "*Corinna's* going a Maying."[15] May morning is set aside for the worship of generative Nature,
so Herrick describes the symbols of the fertility cult:

> Come, my *Corinna*, come; and comming, marke
> How each field turns a street; each street a Parke
> Made green, and trimm'd with trees: see how
> Devotion gives each House a Bough,
> Or Branch: Each Porch, each doore, ere this,
> An Arke a Tabernacle is;

and its amorous realities:

> Many a green-gown has been given;
> Many a kisse, both odde and even:
> Many a glance too has been sent
> From out the eye, Loves Firmament:
> Many a jest told of the Keyes betraying
> This night, and Locks pickt, yet w'are not a Maying.

The tone and attitudes are those of Tibullus.

In "The Country Life," addressed to Endymion Porter, Herrick begins to offer his imitation of the "O fortunatos" passage of Virgil's *Georgics*, book 2, but breaks off after only six verses. The preceding seventy verses are given over to the joys of the gentlemen farmer, free from the vexations and bondage of court and city: "thy Ambition's Master-piece / Flies no thought high then a fleece." As the poet describes the landowner's tour of his estate, he mingles simple observation of a fruitful, well-run farm with, on the one hand, maxims about the value of agriculture to the kingdom, and on the other, the raptures of a pastoral idyll. Then follows a catalog of the seasonal festivals and rustic games that Porter encourages upon his estate, for he was well known as a vigorous supporter of Dover's Cotswold Games. "The Country Life" is one of those early seventeenth-century poems, like "To Penshurst," where pastoral idealization of the country life serves both to compliment an individual person and to embody a social philosophy. Other poems of this kind by Herrick include "A Country Life: To his brother, M. Tho. Herrick" (written ca. 1610) and "A Panegerick to Sir Lewis Pemberton."

Randolph, like Jonson, translated Horace's second epode, but adapted it more to the description of English farm life, and, unlike Jonson, sentimentalized it by omitting the last four verses and replacing them by an unsatirical tag taken from the opening of Horace's sixth satire of the second book. In another poem influenced by Horace he compares his own Horatian calm, content, mental self-sufficiency, and spiritual freedom with the guilt and spiritual slavery of the wealthy enclosing landlord:

> Thou hast a thousand several farms to let,
> And I do feed on ne'er a tenant's sweat.
> Thou has the commons to enclosure brought;
> And I have fix'd no bound to my vast thought.
> What boots it him a large command to have
> Whose every part is some poor vice's slave?[16]

Randolph's regular eclogues include complimentary masquerade, as in "An Eclogues to Mr. Johnson," which includes a debate between poetry and philosophy, and theological allegory, as in "An Eclogue occasioned by Two Doctors disputing upon Predestination," but his characteristic subject matter is erotic, and is typified by such a piece as "A Pastorall Courtship," which is a lubricious rehandling of the theme of the pseudo-Theocritean idyll 27. In his best known poem, "An Ode to Mr. Anthony Stafford to hasten him into the Country," the theme of rural retirement tends toward the amorous, and the poem leans toward Tibullus rather than Horace. Randolph calls his friend away from the City wits who are "Almost at Civil War." For obvious reasons the theme of gentlemanly retirement reached its first considerable prominence in the Civil War and Commonwealth period, but a consideration of the use of that theme in pastoral poetry must await a later chapter.

Chapter Eight
Milton and Marvell

The Horatian motif of rural retirement appears in Milton's most Jonsonian poem, "L'Allegro," which, with its companion-poem, "Il Penseroso," was written probably in 1631–32, and has a place in that large body of Caroline verse in praise of country life. The two poems are seen by H. M. Richmond as belonging to a new genre, "rural lyricism," which is a mutation of the pastoral tradition: "The genre is one of lyrical praise of landscape, spoken at a particular time and place by a more substantial figure than the traditional shepherd—usually the poet in his own person."[1] Thomas Warton the younger, in his edition of Milton's *Poems upon several Occasions* (1785), called "L'Allegro" and "Il Penseroso" "the two first descriptive poems in the English language," and the reader of "L'Allegro" in particular is reminded of the conjectured early meaning of "idyll"—"little picture." Here in a set of lively vignettes the poet conveys a mirthful man's pleasure in observing and involving himself in the "goings-on" of rustic life. He catches the sound of rural labor:

> While the Plowman neer at hand,
> Whistles ore the Furrow'd Land,
> And the Milkmaid singeth blithe,
> And the Mower whets his sithe,
> And every Shepherd tells his tale
> Under the Hawthorn in the dale. (63–68)[2]

(The shepherd telling his tale is, presumably, counting his sheep.) The poet listens also to noises of sport and merrymaking in the countryside: the hounds and hunting horn in the morning, and later some village festival:

When the merry Bells ring round,
And the jocond rebecks sound
To many a youth, and many a maid,
Dancing in the Chequer'd shade;
And young and old com forth to play
On a Sunshine Holyday,
Till the live-long day-light fail,
Then to the Spicy Nut-brown Ale,
With stories told.... (93–101)

These stories are of fairies, the will-o'-the-wisp, and the hobgoblin
Robin Goodfellow, and they are introduced as zestfully and playfully
by Milton as by Browne, Drayton, and Herrick in their comparable
representations of a Merry England, complete with its harmless superstitions.

Two poems written in 1629, but strikingly different from one another in subject and tone, both employ the motifs of classical and
neo-Latin pastoral eclogue. The splendidly pagan Latin elegy 5, "On
the coming of Spring" offers a libertine Golden Age with satyrs roam-
ing in pursuit of coy nymphs, and "Arcadian Pan himself grown
riotous." The deities are symbols, indeed agents, of sexual and generative vitality rushing through the world of external Nature, and Milton
prays that they should remain on earth. By contrast, in the other great
poem of 1629, the ode "On the Morning of Christ's Nativity," Milton,
adopting the medieval patristic notion that pagan gods were demons,
shows them being put to flight at the birth of Christ. In striking
contrast with elegy 5, the natural world is personified here as a
guilty woman "in naked shame / Pollute with sinful blame." Following the Renaissance tradition, this ode Christianizes Virgil's fourth
eclogue, and identifies with the Kingdom of God the age of gold
when Justice (accompanied by Mercy and Truth) will return to men.
Again, Milton follows the Italian neo-Latin fashion of equating Christ
with Pan, the Great Shepherd.

Lycidas[3] was published in 1638, at the end of a volume of Latin,
Greek, and English verse by Cambridge men lamenting the death of
a young graduate-ordinand, Edward King. When *Lycidas* was reprinted in Milton's *Poems* (1645), it carried the explanatory head-
note, "In this Monody the Author bewails a learned Friend, unfortu-
nately drown'd in his Passage from *Chester* on the *Irish* Seas, 1637.

And by occasion foretels the ruin of our corrupted Clergy, then in their height." A monody is a lyric ode sung by a single voice, but after Milton's use of the word here it commonly was used to signify "funeral elegy." *Lycidas* has a regular eclogue form, for, though it opens with the shepherd in full song, the conventional "frame" is supplied by the author speaking in his own voice in the last eight verses, beginning "Thus sang the uncouth Swain." Milton's poem belongs to that well-defined genre shaped by Theocritus's idyll 1, Bion's *Lament for Adonis*, the *Lament for Bion* attributed to Moschus, Virgil's eclogues 5 and 10, and their innumerable Renaissance successors; it is closest both in outline and in specific verbal echoes to Virgil's tenth eclogue, while its ecclesiastical satire belongs to the tradition of Petrarch, Mantuan, and Spenser. Samuel Johnson's notorious hostility to *Lycidas* arose from the very fact that the poem was a pastoral, and so whatever images it could supply were long ago exhausted; but Milton made new these images exhausted by long use in the Renaissance. The very fact that the pastoral convention has a long history

is a part of the meaning it contributes to Milton's poem. The convention pays King the compliment of associating him with the poets for whom Theocritus and Virgil mourned. It assimilates his loss to a long tradition of loss, so that the mystery of the individual occasion is taken up into, and softened by, the general mystery of human fate.[4]

Thus the subject of the elegy is not Edward King merely, but "Lycidas," the peer of Daphnis, Adonis, Gallus, and others, who is furthermore linked in the course of the poem with the Druids (line 53) who were poet-priests, and with Orpheus (58–63) who was the very embodiment of poetic genius. Though the substance of his song is, in great part, the hopes and fears of Milton himself, the shepherd-singer is not simply Milton; this much is made clear by the last eight verses which are in the third person, not the first person of, for instance, Virgil's tenth eclogue. The singer is the type of dedicated poet and is also the common mortal who might share Lycidas's fate (19–22, 75–76). The pastoral world that Lycidas and the poet once inhabited together is not a mere allegory of King and Milton's salad days at Cambridge, but is an image of youth, of innocence, and of a

music close to nature—an image, indeed of all that had been implied
by centuries of pastoral verse:

> Together both, ere the high Lawns appear'd
> Under the opening eye-lids of the morn,
> We drove afield, and both together heard
> What time the Gray-fly winds her sultry horn,
> Batt'ning our flocks with the fresh dews of night,
> Oft still the Star that rose, at Ev'ning bright,
> Toward Heav'ns descent had slop'd his westering wheel.
> Mean while the Rural ditties were not mute,
> Temper'd to th' Oaten Flute,
> Rough *Satyrs* danc'd, and *Fauns* with clov'n heel.   (25–34)

Maynard Mack observes that the depiction of Cambridge life in pastoral terms points to

> a threefold connection between the inspiration of poetry, the sensuous
> appreciation of the natural world, and the intuition of mysterious forces
> (fauns and satyrs) linking poetry and man and nature—which is *truer*
> than would be any of the actual facts of King's and Milton's stay at
> Cambridge.[5]

The shepherd-singer utters a ritual lament in which regular features
of earlier pastoral find their place: the invocation to the Muses, the
appeal to local deities who had failed to save the dead shepherd, the
lament of external nature, the procession of mourners, the flowers
for the (nonexistent) bier, the turn to hope with a realization that
the dead shepherd is immortal. Death and rebirth, death and immortality, were the themes of Bion's *Lament for Adonis* and Virgil's
fifth eclogue; the movement of feeling through Milton's poem is the
usual one from despair to hope—the contrast, that is, between line
8, "For *Lycidas* is dead, dead ere his prime," and line 166, "For
Lycidas your sorrow is not dead"—but this movement is accompanied
by a shift from pagan mythology to Christian.

The subject of the first part of the poem is the shepherd as poet
and his expected reward. Sympathizing external Nature and nymphs
mourn the loss of Lycidas; and the shepherd-singer of the elegy, mind-
ful (lines 19–22) of the possibility of his own early death, asks why,
when death may at any moment take the life of a promising poet and

when a hideous destruction had overtaken even Orpheus the embodiment of poetry itself, should he devote himself to the long study and slow perfection of the poet's craft:

> Were it not better don as others use,
> To sport with *Amaryllis* in the shade,
> Or with the tangles of *Neaera*'s hair?   (67–69)

Amaryllis in Virgil's eclogue 2 is an alternative not to asceticism, toil, and study, but to homosexual love, and her appearance here is typical of Milton's regular practice in this poem, and elsewhere,[6] of dignifying the contexts for his classical allusions. The reply is offered by Phoebus Apollo who, in admonition, touches the poet's trembling ears (line 77) just as he had touched Virgil's to warn him against excessive ambition (eclogue 6, lines 3–4). Phoebus offers an assurance that earthly reputation is insignificant beside the reward of true fame which will be made by "all-judging Jove" (82). This consolation points to a kind of immortality, but remains within a pagan framework of ideas.

The second part of the poem is introduced with a new invocation to the twin founts of pastoral (Aresthusa in the Sicily of Theocritus, and Virgil's native river Mincius), for the preceding passage "was of a higher mood," higher because it treated of the philosophic consolation offered by a prospect of heavenly fame, but also rising to a high pitch of emotional intensity in that menacing "counter-pastoral" image of death's sudden intrusion into all the order, beauty, leisure, and natural harmony that is implied in the pastoral world sketched in lines 25–34: "Comes the blind Fury with th'abhorred shears, / And slits the thin spun life" (75–76).

In the second part of the elegy the conventional device of a procession of mourners is used to introduce St. Peter, who represents the Christian church (not the Church of Rome, which appears in its familiar English pastoral guise as the "grim wolf" of line 127). Milton eagerly seizes an opportunity to use pastoral for its now time-honored purpose of ecclesiastical satire, by placing in St. Peter's mouth a denunciation of Archbishop Laud and his ritualizing "Romish" faction in the Caroline church of England. Here the subject is the shepherd as Christian pastor, so that, in contrast to the first part of the poem, references are to dangers and difficulties in public life rather than in private life; also, questioning of Providence is now more searching:

> How well could I have spar'd for thee young swain,
> Anow of such as for their bellies sake,
> Creep and intrude, and climb into the fold?   (113–15)

Why has God allowed Edward King, potentially a good shepherd, to die, while he allows evil hirelings still to infest his church? The answer is provided by St. Peter himself with image full of menace: "But that two-handed engine at the door, / Stands ready to smite once, and smite no more" (130–31). This engine is an agent of sudden and terrible retribution, though its exact nature might admit, and has admitted, a wide solution.[7]

As the blind Fury earlier had roughly dispelled the pastoral mood, so this second terrible image supplies an abrupt conclusion to a passage of ecclesiastical-allegorical pastoral. In both cases an image of menace shatters the pastoral tone, as Milton, like Virgil in eclogues 1, 9, and 10, allows the timeless pastoral dream to be invaded by the real world of time and loss. After this intrusion a new invocation (lines 132–33) is required, and with it the last reference to the world of pagan pastoral, in a beautiful flower passage. The climax is the apotheosis of Lycidas which is seen in a vision by the shepherd-singer himself; for this time the consolation is not received, as earlier, merely on hearsay from Phoebus or St. Peter. As Lycidas on earth, "under the opening eye-lids of the morn," had moved through a pastoral scene, so now in the eternal morning of immortality he dwells among "other groves and other streams" (171). The true pastoral world is to be found only in heaven. There is a complete and characteristically Renaissance Christianization of the pastoral.

Like *Lycidas*, the slightly longer *Epithaphium Damonis* (1640), a Latin elegy on Charles Diodati, moves from pagan lamentation to Christian hope. Diodati was Milton's close friend, and so not surprisingly this poem has a stronger element of bucolic masquerade than *Lycidas*, but, as in the earlier work, feeling is controlled and ordered by conventions of pastoral. The whole poem is occupied by the lament for Damon, without even a sketchy setting, such as that supplied by the last eight lines of *Lycidas*; though there is something corresponding to the usual eclogue frame in a prefatory prose argument. Milton, under the character of Thyrsis, invokes the Sicilian muse and punctuates his lament with the refrain "Ite domum impasti, domino iam non vacat, agni," "Away, my lambs, unfed, your shepherd heeds you not." This refrain provides a ritual, formal backbone for the poet's reflections upon his loneliness, upon the Italian journey which he was undertaking at the time of his friend's death, and upon his poetic ambitions which he had discussed often before with Diodati. All these unwritten songs Milton was keeping for his friend in the bark of the laurel, "Haec tibi servabam lenta sub cortice lauri" (line 180). Milton–Thyrsis was also keeping for his friend two carved cups given to him by his friend Manso, the distinguished elderly man of letters and patron of Tasso and Marino. These cups are possibly books written by Manso; they recall, of course, the gift that Theocritus's Thyrsis had won by his singing the Lament for Daphnis. The devices on them, which show the phoenix, an emblem of the hope of resurrection, and Amor shooting his arrows up to Heaven as the symbol of Platonic and Christian love, prepare the reader for the conclusion of the poem in an ecstatic vision of Heaven where Damon is a saint and may intercede for Milton–Thyrsis. The elegy ends on this high strain, or, rather, straining after effect—"Festa Sionaeo bacchantur et Orgia Thyrso," "festal orgies rage beneath the thyrsus of Zion"—rather than with the quiet lengthening of perspective, like an evening shadow, in *Lycidas*.

The conclusion of *Lycidas*, "Tomorrow to fresh Woods, and Pastures new," echoes Virgil's "surgamus" in eclogue 10, and similarly implies that the poet will move forward to other kinds of poetry. When Milton moves on to epic, however, he does not altogether abandon pastoral, for the setting of the main action of *Paradise Lost* is not a battlefield, but an earthly paradise which recalls many features of the Golden Age pastoral world of groves, bowers, streams, and flocks, where love is innocent, where man lives in harmony with his environment and nature is responsive to his mood,

> While Universal *Pan*
> Knit with the *Graces* and the Hours in dance
> Led on th'Eternal Spring. (bk. 4, ll. 266–68)

As in *Lycidas*, pagan fable is absorbed into Christian truth:

> Groves whose rich Trees wept odorous Gumms and Balme,
> Others whose fruit, burnisht with Golden Rinde,
> Hung amiable, *Hesperian* Fables true,
> If true, here only.   (bk. 4, ll. 248–51)

The Garden of Eden is a true paradise, unlike pastoral landscapes of pagan myth, but it is a lost paradise. Man can no longer find ideal pastoral harmony with his natural environment now that both are fallen: instead he must fix his hopes upon a heavenly paradise which awaits the faithful (as in *Lycidas*), meanwhile taking comfort from Michael's assurance to Adam that he will possess "A Paradise within thee, happier farr" (bk. 12, l. 587).[8]

A less orthodox "paradise within" is attained by the speaker of "The Garden" by Andrew Marvell (1621–78), whose distinctively witty versions of pastoral were written probably in the 1640s and early 1650s, that is, like Virgil's, against a background of Civil War. In "The Garden" the poet withdraws from a life of ambition and passion. "Garlands of repose" woven by living trees are preferable to symbolic garlands of worldly success, and nature's amorous green is so far preferable to the white and red of beautiful women that "Fair Trees! where s'eer your barkes I wound, / No Name shall but your own be found."[9] This strain of comedy is continued when the poet reverses the meaning of Ovidian fables, to insist that the gods actually wanted the objects of their sexual persecution to be metamorphosed into vegetation:

> *Apollo*, hunted *Daphne* so,
> Only that She might Laurel grow.
> And *Pan* did after *Syrinx* speed,
> Not as a Nymph, but for a Reed.

The poet loves Nature, and, like Simichidas at the conclusion of Theocritus's idyll 7, he luxuriates in her rich abundance:

> What wond'rous Life is this I lead!
> Ripe Apples drop about my head;
> The Luscious Clusters of the Vine
> Upon my Mouth do crush their Wine;
> The Nectaren, and curious Peach,

> Into my hands themselves do reach;
> Stumbling on Melons, as I pass,
> Insnar'd with Flow'rs, I fall on Grass.

Though he stumbles, ensnared, his "fall" is ludicrously much safer than Adam's. From this sensuous delight in the retired garden, the poet retires still farther into a garden of the mind:

> Mean while the Mind, from pleasure less,
> Withdraws into its happiness....
> Annihilating all that's made
> To a green Thought in a green Shade.

This last phrase is a resonant echo of "viridi...umbra" in Virgil's eclogue 9, (line 20), which refers to the poet's creative power: "Who would sing the Nymphs? Who would strew the ground with flowers or cover the fountains with green shade?" Though, as subsequent stanzas of "The Garden" reveal, the soul will one day make a flight to heaven, and though the loss of Eden is to be regretted, the poet can find here and now a paradise within—the pastoral world of the creative imagination itself. Marvell's witty reversal of the Pan and Apollo myths is paralleled by his reversal of the biblical myth: a fall in his garden is the entry to paradise.[10]

Wherever Marvell touches a pastoral convention he plays with it. So for the first twenty-five stanzas of "Daphnis and Chloe" Daphnis appears the ardent, foolish, despairing swain who throws himself into all the metaphorical postures of the courtly lover, but the last two stanzas reveal the reality beneath pastoral masquerades of polite rakes and coquettes:

> But hence Virgins all beware.
> Last night he with *Phlogis* slept;
> This night for *Dorinda* kept;
> And but rid to take the Air.
>
> Yet he does himself excuse;
> Nor indeed without a Cause.
> For, according to the Lawes,
> Why did *Chloe* once refuse?

The "Lawes" are rules established by French Courts of Love, and maintained with various degrees of levity throughout the Renaissance. These laws required the lover to beseech despairingly, and the mistress to be at first disdainful, but at last to yield. Daphnis' appeal to them is anachronistic and cynical, and the poem is resolved into a parody of court-pastoral.

In "A Dialogue between Thyrsis and Dorinda," Thyrsis describes the joys of Elizium in Golden Age terms traditionally employed by Renaissance pastoral poets for descriptions of the Christian heaven. He and Dorinda are so moved by this vision that they innocently decide to commit suicide, and so the poem comes to a distinctly unchristian ending. Where Daphnis is comically oversophisticated, Thyrsis and Dorinda are absurdly simple.

In a group of three, closely linked, love complaints the melancholy swain is no shepherd but a mower. "The Mower to the Glo-Worms" is a neat exercise in hyperbole where the glow-worms' light, illuminating the mower's way home, is outshone by the brilliance of his mistress's beauty:

> Your courteous Lights in vain you wast,
> Since *Juliana* here is come,
> For She my Mind hath so displac'd
> That I shall never find my home.

Displacement of mind suggests, however, something more than conventional lover's despair: it implies a general and unfocused sense of alienation. For all his ingenuousness, the mower has the sophisticated self-consciousness of a philosopher.

"Damon the Mower" takes the conventional eclogue form of song with frame. An introductory stanza enables the poet to distance himself from the despairing lover, to comment ironically (in "seem to paint") upon the fallaciousness of the pathetic fallacy, and to underscore this irony in a series of absurdly trite similes:

> Heark how the Mower *Damon* Sung,
> With love of *Juliana* stung!
> While ev'ry thing did seem to paint
> The Scene more fit for his complaint.
> Like her fair Eyes the day was fair;
> But scorching like his am'rous Care.

> Sharp like his Sythe his Sorrow was,
> And wither'd like his Hopes the Grass.

Damon's song, like so many other English pastoral love complaints, is modeled distantly upon Virgil's eclogue 2. There is a positive echo of Virgil's "nec sum adeo informis," with its recollection of Theocritus' idyll 11, in the first verse of Marvell's eighth stanza:

> Nor am I so deform'd to sight,
> If in my Sithe I looked right;
> In which I see my Picture done,
> As in a crescent Moon the Sun.
> The deathless Fairyes take me oft
> To lead them in their Danses soft;
> And, when I tune my self to sing,
> About me they contract their Ring.

Marvell has wittily re-created a latter-day English Polyphemus—a grotesque in the distorting mirror of his scythe, a giant among fairies, who, when he throws "his Elbow round, / Depopulating all the Ground" with his scythe, is as violent and destructive as Polyphemus too. The mower brings gifts to his shepherdess stranger than those offered by the Cyclops to Galatea:

> To Thee the harmless Snake I bring,
> Disarmed of its teeth and sting.
> To Thee *Chameleons* changing-hue,
> And oak leaves tipt with hony due.

Damon is so absurdly clumsy as to cut his own ankle, "By his own Sythe, the Mower mown," but he heals this hurt with herbs traditionally used by rustics, and—true would-be pastoral lover that he is—he declares that his shepherdess's eyes have wounded him more severely:

> Alas! said He, these hurts are slight
> To those that dye by Loves despight.
> With Shepherds-purse, and Clowns-all-heal,
> The Blood I stanch, and Wound I seal.
> Only for him no Cure is found,
> Whom *Julianas* Eyes do wound.

> 'Tis death alone that this must do:
> For Death thou art a Mower too.

The last line, which balances on a knife-edge between portentousness and absurdity, again reveals the mower as a philosopher of sorts.

In the third love complaint, "The Mower's Song," the mower recalls the harmony he once enjoyed with fresh and gay meadows, where his mind, "in the greenness of the Grass / Did see its Hopes as in a Glass." After this mirror image (cf. Spenser's *Januarye*), the second stanza reverses the terms of the pathetic fallacy, and the mower observes that while he pines with unrequited love the meadows unsympathetically continue to grow more luxuriant. So in revenge he will take his scythe, "And Flow'rs, and Grass, and I and all, / Will in one common Ruine fall." "The Mower's Song" has a refrain, the rhythm of which is compared by H. M. Margoliouth to "the long regular sweep of the scythe":[11] "When *Juliana* came [For *Juliana* comes], and She / What I do to the Grass, does to my thoughts and Me." Such a distinction between thoughts and me, like the reference to displacement of mind in "The Mower to the Glo-Worms," suggests that the mower's real problem is self-consciousness. As Donald Friedman argues, "the great subject of all the 'Mower' poems is the impossible reconciliation between man and the world of natural creation of which he is a part. The mind may mirror the order of the world, but it is the imagination that divides man ultimately from the field of that imagination."[12]

A fourth poem in which a mower is the speaker may be considered here. "The Mower against Gardens" is a witty piece of dialectic on the opposition between Nature and Art. The mower asserts the vitality and innocence of uncultivated external nature against the forced art of artificial flower propagation in a formal garden. Nature here is that pastoral landscape of Drayton and Herrick, haunted by English fairies and classic fauns:

> 'Tis all enforc'd; the Fountain and the Grot;
>   While the sweet Fields do lye forgot:
> Where willing Nature does to all dispence
> A wild and fragrant Innocence:
> And *Fauns* and *Faryes* do the Meadows till,
>   More by their presence than their skill.

> Their Statues polish'd by some ancient hand,
> May to adorn the Gardens stand:
> But howso'ere the Figures do excel,
> The *Gods* themselves with us do dwell.

In this distinction between gods and statues the fruitful spirit of nature is opposed to mere forms of art. The speaker is not, however, the creative, imaginative poet (as in "The Garden"), but that strange, unsettling, absurd philosopher, the Mower.

The garden, the fields, and the mower reappear in a central episode of "Upon Appleton House, to my Lord Fairfax," the most elaborate English estate poem in the Martial–Jonson tradition. The poem is a panegyric upon the Fairfax family, and, in particular, upon the general's daughter Maria, to whom Marvell was tutor. Its climax, stanzas 82–96, portrays nature's homage to the girl in an elaboration of that pastoral hyperbole of Virgil's eclogue 7 by which nature's beauties are seen to depend on the presence of the beloved:

> *She* streightness on the Woods bestows;
> To *Her* the Meadow sweetness owes;
> Nothing could make the River be
> So Chrystal-pure but only *She*;
> *She* yet more Pure, Sweet, Streight, and Fair,
> Then Gardens, Woods, Meads, Rivers are. (stanza 87)

By her presence the Appleton estate becomes a modern Tempe, a living Elizium, a more chaste Idalian Grove and a map of Paradise (stanzas 95, 96); but the fields are still recognizably the English workaday landscape of an open-field village where, after haymaking, the meadow is grazed in common:

> The Villagers in common chase
> Their Cattle, which it closer rase;
> And what below the Sith increast
> Is pincht yet nearer by the Beast. (stanza 57)

The haymakers are idyllic figures, in a simple, harmonious relationship with nature:

> Where every Mowers wholesome Heat
> Smells like an *Alexanders sweat*

> Their Females fragrant as the Mead
> Which they in *Fairy Circles* tread:
> When at their Dances End they kiss,
> Their new-made Hay not sweeter is. . . .   (stanza 54)

Their activities are a harmless and fruitful contrast to the Civil War
that has just raged over paradisal England:

> The Mower now commands the Field;
> In whose new Traverse seemeth wrought
> A Camp of Battail newly fought:
> Where, as the Meads with Hay, the Plain
> Lyes quilted ore with Bodies slain:
> The Women that with forks it fling,
> Do represent the Pillaging.   (stanza 53)

Even haymaking is not without its violence, however, by which the
innocent suffer; for to his dismay a mower kills a rail, or corncrake,
with his scythe (stanza 50). The allegory of the Civil War and execu-
tion of the king is not forced, but is undoubtedly present,[13] and throws
into relief the blessed retiredness of the poet which is described in
ensuing stanzas (61–78). As in the conclusion of Theocritus's idyll
7, the poet is easefully involved in the scene:

> Then, languishing with ease, I toss
> On Pallets swoln of Velvet Moss;
> While the Wind, cooling through the Boughs,
> Flatters with Air my panting Brows.   (stanza 75)

But Marvell, typically, emphasizes the distinction between mind and
body even as he writes of a mental security which complements his
physical ease: "How safe, methinks, and strong, behind / These Trees
have I incamp'd my Mind" (stanza 76). Despite the rage of Civil
War and the trivial, ordinary, yet disturbing violence of the hay-
field, Marvell has found, if not quite a paradise within, at least a
safe stronghold.

All Marvell's versions of pastoral, whether they take the form of
"rural lyricism," as in "The Garden," or country-house panegyric, or
Arcadian shepherd dialogue, are highly original; but his most distinctive contribution to pastoral's continuing debate about man's

relationship with external nature is through his creation of that culti-vator-destroyer, the mower—an amazingly sophisticated Polyphemus figure, who has no successor in the English pastoral tradition.

Chapter Nine

Restoration and Augustan

As Virgil created an harmonious pastoral world in the teeth of the almost unbearable disorder of Roman Civil Wars, so Marvell's "The Garden" and "Upon Appleton House" assert the values of rural retirement and contemplation in the face of English Civil War. Not surprisingly, the 1640s and 1650s saw a large crop of English "retirement poems" written, understandably enough, mostly by committed Royalists, rather than by half-committed Parliamentarians such as Marvell.

In Sir John Denham's *Cooper's Hill* (1642) we find the pastoral opposition of city and country, when the avarice, noise, dirt, and Puritan fanaticism of London are contrasted with the beauty, security, and innocence of the countryside. Thus an implicitly idyllic current runs from the very fountainhead of "local poetry."[1] The Civil War adds an edge to otherwise undistinguished commonplaces in, for instance, "To Retiredness" in the *Otia Sacra* (1648) of Mildmay Fane, second earl of Westmoreland: "Thus out of fears, or noise of Warr ... I hugg my Quiet." Iron times of war validate a view of the workday English countryside as an emblem of the Golden Age,

> Then turning over Nature's leaf,
> I mark the Glory of the Sheaf,
> For every Field's a severall page,
> Disciphering the Golden Age ...

but poetry of retirement had no need of any factional edge supplied by the opposition between Parliamentary-Puritan-City and Royalist-Anglican-Countryside. Pastoral tradition, including Virgil's *Georgics* and Horace, encouraged writers to glorify, and gentlemen to reside in, an English countryside just coming into its brief golden age of beauty between medieval wildness and industrial squalor. Thus, from the middle years of the seventeenth to the early years of the nineteenth centuries, we find among the more delightful minor poets a line of country squires who sought to shape their estates, their verses, and their lives upon models sketched by Horace, Virgil, and Martial.

Charles Cotton (1630–87), whose occasional verse was published in 1689, is an early and attractive example of his type. He wrote pastoral eclogues and an imitation of Marlowe's "Passionate Shepherd to his Love" where, denying Ralegh's assumption that the pastoral world must be a perpetual summer, he broadens his lover's appeal to include the delights and offerings of winter. He wrote charming descriptions in the "L'Allegro," rural-lyric vein in his "Quatrains" celebrating morning, noon, evening, and night, where he catches the sights and sounds of a summer's day in the countryside: folk going to work in the fields; a waggoner lugging his load as the harness of the leading horse jingles impatiently; pans and bowls newly scalded and reared up against the wall of the milking-shed. He takes an unceasing delight in the "goings-on" of ordinary country life, and with his closely detailed rural observation he mingles classical pastoral allusion easily and unself-consciously. Thus, alongside sobbing Philomel he hears the booming bittern, while the long evening shadow of a boy driving the sheep to fold makes him appear "a mighty *Polypheme*." Cotton is best known as author of the second part added to the 1676 edition of Walton's *The Compleat Angler*, the most popular prose idyll in the English language; and it was here that his irregular stanzas "The Retirement" were first printed. In this poem Cotton says farewell to the busy world, and luxuriates in the sweetness, innocence, beauty, and peace of the Derbyshire Dove where he loved to ply his angle. Beresford Hall and the River Dove complement Horace's Sabine Farm and Fons Bandusiae, but Cotton's conception of idyllic retirement is satisfying because so firmly rooted in the realities of the country life of his class and period.

The "retirement poem" represents a new and fruitful mid-seventeenth-century development of the pastoral idyll of the good life: other forms of pastoral—amatory, popular, and allegorical—continued by and large in pre–Civil War forms. Simple, apparently "artless" pastoral songs and ballads of the Elizabethan kind were still being written, and many of them were published in the song books compiled by John Playford (1623–86) and his son Henry. Others, generally of a more bawdy kind, appeared in a series of "Drolleries" between 1656 and 1672. *Covent-Garden Drollery* (1672) may be taken as typical: apart from a few prologues and epilogues to plays, one or two satires and drinking songs, this collection is wholly pastoral and amatory. There are willow garlands and poor shepherds dying of love, but "dying" more commonly carries a sexual connotation, as in Dryden's "Whilst Alexis lay prest" reprinted from *Marriage-a-la Mode.* Shepherds and nymphs are town-rakes and their women, but occasionally boorish country lovers are introduced for comic effect. A patronizing sub-Herrick kind of writing appears in "A rural dance at a Shropshire Wake"; but much closer to the countryside is that famous maypole song "Come lasses and lads, take leave of your dads" which was printed in *Westminster Drolleries,* part 2 (1672), and later in *Pills to Purge Melancholy* and many other song books.

The most prolific and popular writer and editor of pastoral songs was Tom D'Urfey (1653–1723), compiler of *Wit and Mirth, or Pills to Purge Melancholy* (1699–1720). In that anthology, prewar, and even sixteenth-century wooing dialogues, songs in praise of milk-maids and husbandmen, and celebrations of rural festivals reappear, alongside more recent songs of rural frolicking, such as "The Green Gown" and D'Urfey's own verses in the "pastourelle" tradition such as "A Shepherd kept Sheep on a Hill so High."[2] Song books were a meeting place of popular culture and the court; for in the late seventeenth century the connection between the songs of the common people and learned or aristocratic art was even closer than it had been under the first two Stuarts. Walter Pope (1625?–1714), professor of astronomy and Fellow of the Royal Society, wrote a jolly retirement poem "The Wish" (1684) which earned great popularity as a broadside ballad. Charles Sackville, earl of Dorset (1643–1706), collected popular ballads and wrote in ballad form: something of the crudeness of a street ballad appears in, for instance, his satire upon pastoral courtly love:

> Phillis the fairest of Love's foes....
> So long she kept her legs so close
> Till they had scarce a rag on.[3]

Amatory pastoral, both popular and courtly, was more indecent than pre–Civil War: nowhere more so than in the pastorals of John Wilmot, earl of Rochester (1647–80), which range from bawdy trifling, in "Fair *Cloris* in a Pig-Stye lay," to pungent satire in "A Ramble in St. James's Park," where the love-game played in pastoral masquerade by the *beau monde* is seen for what it really is, and the nymph Corinna is a bitch with three curs at her tail. As Rochester's friend Sir Charles Sedley observed, "Our Arcadia is Hyde Park and the Mulberry Garden." In the character of Strephon, Rochester wrote a few conventional amatory pastoral dialogues and songs, but his ghost may well have taken a wry view of the pastoral elegy (1681) upon his death by Thomas Flatman:[4]

> As on his Death-bed gasping Strephon lay,
> *Strephon* the wonder of the Plains,
> The noblest of the Arcadian Swains.

That Flatman was more usefully employed in his translations from Horace is confirmed by his "On the Death of Mr. Pelham Humfries: Pastoral Song":

> Did you not hear the hideous groan,
> The shrieks, and heavy moan
> That spread themselves o'er all the pensive plain;
> And rent the breast of many a tender swain?
> 'Twas for Amintas, dead and gone.

Flatman is not worse than most: the grisly work of pastoral elegists between 1650 and 1800 must have added materially to the terror of death for the great and not-so-great.

After *Lycidas* conventional pastoral elegy and eclogue effectively died to be resurrected only briefly by Pope, and pastoral vitality flowed into other forms; but paradoxically only when the conventional forms were moribund did a vigorous critical debate[5] on the nature of pastoral begin, with the English translation in 1684 of Rapin's *Dissertatio de Carmine Pastorali* (1659), and in 1695 of Fontenelle's *Discours sur la nature de l'eclogue* (1688). Rapin regarded pastoral as an imitation of the actions of shepherds living in a remote or fictitious golden age, whereas Fontenelle saw pastoral as

simply a representation of the peacefulness of rural life. In practice
pastorals written according to one theory would not be very different
from those written according to the other; but Rapin claimed to
have derived his rules from the ancients, whereas Fontenelle claimed
to have formulated *his* rules by the "Natural Light" of his own
reason; so the dispute between the two critics became an episode in
the late seventeenth-century "Battle of the Books" between ancients
and moderns.

A critical theory of pastoral based upon Fontenelle but ultimately
going beyond him in the matter of pastoral's truth to contemporary
reality was given a wide hearing and a touch of party political bias
in the *Spectator* and the *Guardian,* where Whig critics extravagantly
praised the pastorals of Ambrose Philips (1674–1749) and studiously
ignored those of Pope. Addison in *Spectator,* no. 523 (1712), praising Philips for having banished the whole tribe of rural deities in
favor of the real superstitions of contemporary English country folk,
claimed that he had "given a new life and a more natural beauty"
to pastoral poetry. Addison's protegé Thomas Tickell, in *Guardian,*
nos. 22, 23, 28, 30 and 32 in 1713, followed Addison's line, extravagantly praised Philips, and argued that pastoral poetry should be true
to contemporary reality while bestowing a tint of easy contentment
on country life, emphasizing what is agreeable and hiding what is
wretched. In number 22 he declared that the appeal of pastoral lies
in its readers' "secret approbation of natural goodness"; thus a link
was formed between pastoral criticism and the traditional theory of
"natural man" now newly fashionable in the writings of the third
earl of Shaftesbury. Tacitus saw gleams of natural virtue in the Ger-
mans; Horace, Virgil, and Cicero praised the simple Scythians; Montaigne the cannibals; but Shaftesbury, as publicist of the Cambridge
Platonists' ideas, spread widely the notion of innate virtue and its
corollary—that vice existed only where natural goodness had been
corrupted by education, by luxury, and by all that is known as
civilization.

Critical theory generally has lagged behind poetic practice. The
Guardian writer was calling for nothing very revolutionary in view
of the writings of Spenser, Drayton, Browne, and many other pre–
Civil War pastoralists; and when Ambrose Philips included English
scenery, folklore, and dialect in his *Pastorals* (the first of which were
published in *Oxford and Cambridge Miscellany Poems,* 1706) he

was merely doing indifferently well the kind of thing that had been done very well before. Philips's pastorals would hardly be remembered had not Pope ridiculed their "pretty rusticity" in his gleefully ironic *Guardian*, no. 40. In fact they are not nearly as rustic as Pope claims; so that when he wishes to ridicule what he asserts is Philips's Theocritean "Doric" diction he has to quote the opening lines of Spenser's *September*, not a passage from Philips.

Pope's critical position had already been outlined in "A Discourse on Pastoral Poetry" written, or at least first drafted, in 1704, but not to be published until 1717. It is based principally upon Rapin but incorporates ideas from Fontenelle:

> pastoral is an image of what they call the Golden age. So that we are not to describe our shepherds as shepherds at this day really are, but as they may be conceiv'd then to have been; when the best of men follow'd the employment. . . .[6]

Pope's own four pastorals, first published alongside Ambrose Philips's in *Tonson's Poetical Miscellanies, The Sixth Part* (1709), brilliantly exemplify his neoclassic theory. As his "Discourse" makes clear, they were intended to summarize and complete the tradition of classical pastoral: "these four comprehend all the subjects which the Critics upon *Theocritus* and *Virgil* will allow to be fit for pastoral." They cover the four seasons of the year and the times of day and settings previously encountered in pastoral: thus spring, early morning in a valley; summer, a river bank at noon; autumn, a hill at sunset; and winter, a pine grove at night. They cover the typical kinds, as song-contest, uncompetitive dialogue, love-complaint, and elegy. The models are first Virgil and second Theocritus, with echoes of Spenser, Bion, Moschus, and occasionally Waller, Congreve, and other Restoration poets. Pope's frame of reference is wholly literary: thus "A Milk-white Bull shall at your Altars stand, / That threats a Fight, and spurns the rising Sand" ("Spring," ll. 47–48) comes from Virgil's eclogue 3, lines 86–87.

> See what Delights in Sylvan Scenes appear!
> Descending Gods have found *Elysium* here.
> In Woods bright *Venus* with *Adonis* stray'd,
> And chast *Diana* haunts the Forest Shade
> ("Summer," ll. 59–62)

is derived from Virgil's eclogues 2, line 60, and 10, line 18; and so on. Pope even attempts the syntactical tightness of Latin, where sentence structure becomes clear only with the concluding verb: "Celestial *Venus* haunts *Idalia*'s Groves, / *Diana Cynthus, Ceres Hybla* loves" ("Spring," ll. 65–66). The reader's attention is caught as much by verbal patterning, the dance of syntax, as by the substance of Pope's thought or the progress of his narrative. In the following couplet an inverted order of terms (Rocks, Caves, *Delia, Delia*, Cave, Rock) enacts the beating of an echo back and forth: "Thro' Rocks and Caves the Name of *Delia* sounds, / *Delia*, each Cave and echoing Rock rebounds" ("Autumn," ll. 49–50). The couplet re-creates on a limited, indeed Lilliputian, scale the effect of Sidney's double sestina (see chap. 4) in dramatizing the idea of a closed world of love-longing, but the patterned art, the purely verbal activity, is most immediately striking.

Pope's art consistently draws attention to itself, whether as verbal music or as verbal painting. In the prefatory "Discourse" he promised that in each eclogue "a design'd scene or prospect is to be presented to our view." The primary sense of "scene" in Pope's day referred to painted stage scenery, while "prospect" was a painter's term too. Landscapes in the *Pastorals* are composed in painterly terms:

> Here where the *Mountains* less'ning as they rise,
> Lose the low Vales, and steal into the Skies.
> While lab'ring Oxen, spent with Toil and Heat,
> In their loose Traces from the Field retreat;
> While curling Smokes from Village-Tops are seen,
> And the fleet Shades glide o'er the dusky Green.
>   ("Autumn," ll. 59–64)

The mind's eye is directed from background to foreground to middle ground, giving the effect of a picture seen from a fixed viewpoint, even though the scene is animated, notably in "rise," "Lose," "steal," and that perfect suiting of sound to sense in line 64. Music and painting similarly come together in the following:

> Soon as the Flocks shook off the nightly Dews,
> Two Swains, whom Love kept wakeful, and the Muse,

Pour'd o'er the whitening Vale their fleecy Care,
Fresh as the Morn, and as the Season fair:
The dawn now blushing on the Mountain's Side.
("Spring," ll. 17–21)

Geoffrey Tillotson analyzes the musical balance and variety: "There is no antithesis [in line 18] between the swains, although they are two. But their sleep is troubled by two things and these are so used as to make balance possible.... [Line 20] shows an inversion of music but not an inversion of meaning: the half-lines are parallel in meaning but inverted in music."[7] Jeffry Spencer comments upon pictorial effects, and likens the passage to Venetian rococo art: "The sheep, a mass of vivid white in the clear morning sunlight, are 'pour'd' over the vale while, in the distance, the mountainside reflects the pinkish tones of the dawn sky. As in Zuccarelli's work, domestic animals are used decoratively."[8]

Pope triumphantly asserts the value of artificiality, but his *Pastorals* are not without moral substance. The last of his many echoes of Virgil's *Eclogues*, near the end of his *Pastorals*, introduces a significant variation:

But see, *Orion* sheds unwholsome Dews,
Arise, the Pines a noxious Shade diffuse;
Sharp *Boreas* blows, and Nature feels Decay,
Time conquers All, and We must Time obey.
("Winter," ll. 85–88)

"Arise" translates Virgil's resonant "surgamus" (eclogue 10, line 75), and the rest of line 86 echoes Virgil's reference to the harmfulness of shade. Line 88 translates the last verse of Gallus's song (eclogue 10, line 69), "Omnia vincit Amor: et nos cedamus Amori," with the all-important substitution of "Time" for "Love," because Pope's organizing theme is the fleetingness of human life. The comment Pope made upon Spenser's *The Shepheardes Calender* may be applied to his own *Pastorals*: "he compares human Life to the several Seasons, and at once exposes to his readers a view of the great and little worlds." The correspondence between human life and external nature is in a common mortality: "Nature feels decay." Pope's tiny calendar of four brief pastorals lacks the moral complexity and weight, the metrical and linguistic variety, and the developed self-characterization of *The Shepheardes Calender*; but in so considerable a scaling-down of Spenser's scheme Pope perhaps emphasizes the brevity of life, as compared with the long endurance of art, and certainly, like Spenser, he absorbs a whole literary tradition and fixes it in a single, monumental work of art.

A critical debate on the nature of pastoral poetry continued through the eighteenth century but the theory sketched in Pope's "Discourse" attracted progressively fewer adherents. Most critics contented themselves with only the broadest definitions of pastoral poetry: Johnson, in *Rambler*, no. 37 (1750), concluded "Whatsoever, therefore, may, according to the common course of things, happen in the country, may afford a subject for a Pastoral Poet"; for Goldsmith its subject was "something in the Pastoral or rural life; and the persons, or interlocuters, introduced in it, either shepherds or other rusticks."[9] Pastoral poetry thus conceived could be cast into the traditional classical mold of the eclogue, into the more highly esteemed georgic kind, into dramatic, and into less clearly defined narrative, descriptive, or lyrical forms, including the relatively new ones of "retirement poetry" and "local poetry."

Johnson observed in *Rambler*, no. 135 (1751), "There is, indeed, scarcely any writer who has not celebrated the happiness of rural privacy;"[10] and so pervasive is the retirement theme that it comes as no surprise to find at the end of the century that sociable, utterly urbane city banker Samuel Rogers trilling "Mine be a cot beside the hill" (1782).

In miscellanies and magazines a horde of poets continued to twitter away rhythmically, in the *England's Helicon* tradition, to Phillis and Delia, or, increasingly, to a scarcely distinguishable Molly or Kate; but the long-felt absurdity of pastoral love-complaint was effectively ridiculed by Swift in "A Love-Song in the Modern Taste" (*Gentleman's Magazine*, June 1733):

> Mild *Arcadians*, ever blooming,
>   Nightly nodding o'er your Flocks,
> See my weary Days consuming,
>   All beneath yon flow'ry Rocks....
> Melancholly smooth *Meander*,

> Swiftly purling in a Round,
> On thy Margin Lovers wander,
> With thy flow'ry Chaplets crown'd.

A subgenre of pastoral lyric, the "Pastoral Ballad" in anapaestic measure, became prominent in miscellany and magazine verse after Addison had printed and praised John Byrom's (1692–1763) "Pastoral" in *Spectator*, no. 603. One of these, "Colin's Complaint" by Nicholas Rowe (1673–1718), was set to a popular tune, printed as a broadside in 1713, and included in the 1720 supplementary volume to D'Urfey's *Pills to Purge Melancholy*, in Ramsay's *The Tea-Table Miscellany*, and in many other song books. The most celebrated was Shenstone's "Pastoral Ballad," first printed in the *London Magazine*, December 1751, but later greatly enlarged into the familiar and often reprinted four-part version. Shenstone's piece is perfect in its very limited, delightfully artificial, way:

> My banks, they are furnish'd with bees,
> Whose murmur invites one to sleep;
> My waters are shaded with trees,
> And my hills are white over with sheep.

What appears to be an attempt to "naturalize" this form slightly appears in the pastoral ballads on the four seasons by Thomas Brerewood (d. 1748), where the settings are deliberately unidyllic. Thus "Autumn" (*Gentleman's Magazine*, September 1754):

> When the ways are so miry, that bogs they might seem,
> And the axle-tree's ready to break,
> While the waggoner whistles in stopping his team,
> And then claps the poor jades on the neck.

Pastoral eclogues written in obedience to Pope's theory and Virgil's all too distant example produced a thick, if hardly healthy, crop in the eighteenth century in the work of Blacklock, Byrom, Duck, Fenton, Hammond, (it is a dispiriting list), Logan, Lyttelton, William Thompson, and their numerous like. This work is the metrical counterpart to portrait paintings of fashionable ladies as Pastora, such as Nell Gwynne with a shepherd's crook and an elaborate coiffure, or the rage for dairies that the duchess of Bedford brought back from

Madame de Pompadour's court. At its best such verse achieves a wan charm, at its worst the "frigid pedantry" that Johnson anathemized in Hammond's verse.

The eclogue was still used for nonpastoral purposes.[11] The example of Sannazaro's piscatorical eclogues prompted William Diaper (1686?–1717) to write his *Nereides or Sea Eclogues* (1712). Somewhat closer to the "rural sports" type of georgic is the *Angling Sports, in Nine Piscatory Eclogues* (1729) by Moses Browne (1704–87). An extension of the eclogue into another rural sport was provided by the delightful and too little known *Partridge-Shooting, an Eclogue* (1767) by Francis Fawkes (1720–77) who was the author of a very influential translation of Theocritus published in the same year. However, there is little, apart from its length, to distinguish Fawkes's eclogue from the rural sports georgics of, for instance, Gay and Somervile.

The "town eclogue," a more common eighteenth-century form, can, like the piscatory, be traced back to Theocritus—in this case, to idyll 15. The Theocritean original itself was imitated in a free and lively fashion by Robert Lloyd (1733–64) as "Chit-Chat." Swift wrote "A Town Eclogue" in 1710 consisting of the dialogue of a prostitute and her client. Poems of this kind written in the following decade by Pope, John Gay (1685–1732) and Lady Mary Wortley Montagu (1689–1762) were published together as *Six Town Eclogues* (1747). "City Eclogues" and "Town Eclogues" proliferated in miscellanies and magazines. There were prison eclogues and suburban eclogues, and even "The Billingsgate Contest, a Piscatory London Eclogue, in Imitation of the Third Eclogue of Virgil" (*Gentleman's Magazine*, May 1734).

The eclogue continued in use for compliment. As late as 1798 (*Gentleman's Magazine*, July) we find "A Congratulatory Pastoral on the Arrival of Sir Sidney Smith" with Damon and Moeris as interlocutors. But the form found a readier use for satire, in such political pieces as "The Squire and the Parson" (1748) by Soame Jenyns, "The Prophecy of Famine, a Scots Pastoral" (1763) by Charles Churchill, or "The Dean and the Squire, a Political Eclogue" (1782) by William Mason. On the level of personal lampoon there were pieces such as "Bozzy and Piozzi, or the British Biographers, a Town Eclogue" (1786) by Wolcot.

The line of the religious eclogue was continued by Pope's "Messiah, a Sacred Eclogue, in imitation of Virgil's Pollio" (first printed in the *Spectator*, no. 378 [1712]) which was widely imitated. Faintly related to this type is a Swedenborgian rigmarole by William Gilbert, *The Hurricane, a Theosophical and Western Eclogue* (1796). American passages in this work relate it to the exotic eclogues—"American," "Oriental," "African," "Arabian," "Eastern"—that followed the publication in 1742 of the *Persian Eclogues* of William Collins (1721–59).

Chapter Ten

Naturalized Pastoral

Collins and his successors were casting around for fresh kinds of pastoral. The main stream lay however in the direction indicated by the *Guardian*; and paradoxically a friend of Pope was the first to meet the Whig critics' call for indigenous pastoral eclogue. Abel Evans (1679–1737) who, if remembered at all, is remembered as an epigrammatist, wrote pastorals set in ordinary English village society and, alongside the "amorous pains" of conventional pastoral, displayed some of the real discomforts and satisfactions, and some of the true commonsense philosophy of the herdsman:

> All wet and weary William home return'd
> From distant fairs, and o'erstock'd markets mourn'd.
> Slowly lag on his weather-beaten fold,
> The greater part as yet remain'd unsold....
> William
> Sure I set out on some unlucky day!
> But, coming fairs my pains may better pay.
> 'Twere vain to grieve; what must be will befall;
> Good and ill hap, by turn, still wait on all.
> Now, say the news, e'er since I saw thee last,
> And how the Whitsun holidays were past;
> Who won the wrestling prizes at the wake;
> Whose head was broke, and for what lass's sake;
> Hath lovesome Lobin wedded buxom Kate?
> And how doth Roger bear his high estate?
> Roger turn'd farmer! Plow-boys, prick your ears!
> What lubber now to make his fortune fears?
> (Pastoral 3, ll. 1–4, 17–28)

The very flatness of Evans's recital of commonplaces is appropriate to his aim, which is to fit the shepherds of literary pastoral into actual social and economic relationships of village society. Evans wrote pastorals between 1707 and 1726 but none was published until six of them appeared in *Nichol's Select Collection of Miscellaneous Poems* (1782).

It was John Gay, another friend of Pope, who brought the debate on "naturalized" English pastoral to a fruitful stage with his *The Shepherd's Week* (1714); but Gay's first poetry of rural life was a georgic, *Rural Sports*. The English georgic line had recently begun with *Cyder* (1708) where John Philips (1676–1709), like Virgil, combined a painstakingly realistic account of husbandry with an appealing dream of the innocence, felicity, vigor, and piety of the ideal happy husbandman's life. The climax of *Cyder* is a vision of plenty which shows England's power abroad as a reflex of the joys of harvest-home and the "transporting prospect" of rich fields and villages where sturdy laborers enjoy their ale and wheaten bread. Throughout the eighteenth century the georgic sang of a Merry England bursting with well-being, a rural counterpart to Hogarth's Beer Street.

This patriotism animates Gay's *Rural Sports* (1713; revised 1720) with its "happy plains," "bulging barns," and "happy fields, unknown to noise and strife . . . the kind rewarders of industrious life." ("Happy" recalls a key word in Virgil's *Georgics*—"laetus," which implies fertility divinely and especially bestowed to reward the husbandmen's industry.) Gay's principal subjects are the retired gentleman's country sports, but the poet intersperses his accounts of coursing, hunting, fowling, and angling with a series of vignettes displaying the healthful, useful labor of hardy, temperate, contented country folk; and the climax of his poem in its 1720 version is a rapturously sentimental account, modeled on Virgil's "O fortunatos," of the cottager's wife:

> What happiness the rural maid attends,
> In chearful labour while each day she spends!
> She gratefully receives what heav'n has sent,
> And, rich in poverty, enjoys content.[1]

The Shepherd's Week was partly the outcome of the Pope–Philips quarrel. By low comedy and broad indelicacy, and by a laborious "Alphabetical Catalogue of Names, Plants, Flowers, Fruits, Birds, Beasts, Insects, and other material things mentioned," Gay mocks

the Whig critics' call for realism; while in the archaisms and allitera-
tions of his "Proeme to the Courteous Reader" (a parody of E. K.'s
scholia), and in annotations to the eclogues themselves, he ridicules
not only Philips but Theocritus and Spenser too. The "Proeme" is a
piece of grave fooling which opens ridiculously:

Great marvell hath it been (and that not unworthily) to diverse worthy
wits, that in this our Island of Britain, in all rare sciences so greatly
abounding, more especially in all kinds of Poesie highly flourishing, no
Poet (though otherways of notable cunning in roundelays) hath hit on
the right simple Eclogue after the true ancient guise of Theocritus before this mine attempt.

Gay writes ironically behind the mask of a self-important, blundering,
"Modern" pastoralist. He praises Theocritus because he "maketh his
Louts give foul Language, and behold their Goats at Rut in all sim-
plicity," and duly in one of his own eclogues shows a village wench
Marian, in all simplicity, overseeing the parson's bull as it serves
Goody Dobbin's cow. Even so, Marian is not altogether the object
of Gay's ridicule. In some respects she is as sympathetic a character
as the cottager's wife in *Rural Sports*:

> *Marian*, that soft could stroke the udder'd cow,
> Or lessen with her sieve the barley mow;
> Marbled with sage the hard'ning cheese she press'd,
> And yellow butter *Marian's* skill confess'd.
> ("Tuesday," ll. 11–14)

Specific pastoral parody in *The Shepherd's Week* is directed more
against Virgil than against Theocritus; so in the description by Bowze-
beus of the country man's holiday in "Saturday" Gay offers his absurdly
"naturalized" parallel to Virgil's eclogue 6:

> Now he goes on, and sings of fairs and shows,
> For still new fairs before his eyes arose.
> How pedlar's stalls with glitt'ring toys are laid,
> The various fairings of the country maid.
> Long silken laces hang upon the twine,
> And rows of pins and amber bracelets shine;

> How the tight lass, knives, combs, and scissors spys,
> And looks on thimbles with desiring eyes.
> Of lott'ries next with tuneful note he told,
> Where silver spoons are won and rings of gold.
> The lads and lasses trudge the street along,
> And all the fair is crowded in his song.
> The mountebank now treads the stage, and sells
> His pills, his balsams, and his ague-spells;
> Now o'er and o'er the nimble tumbler springs,
> And on the rope the ventrous maiden swings;
> *Jack Pudding* in his parti-colour'd jacket
> Tosses the glove, and jokes at ev'ry packet.
> Of *Raree-shows* he sung, and *Punch's* feats,
> Of pockets pick'd in crowds, and various cheats.   (71–90)

This "realism," however, captures vividly and sympathetically the actual gaiety of the country fair; so that the final effect is not altogether that of burlesque.

Despite the irony of his "Proeme," Gay stands alongside Theocritus, not opposed to him. *The Shepherd's Week* is a burlesque in Theocritean vein, gaining its effect by a discrepancy between coarse matter and elegant manner. Devices of refined art shape material of common life into an order that it conspicuously fails to have in actuality; for instance, assonance and tactful alliteration in the moanings of a bereaved lover in "Friday":

> If by the dairy's hatch I chance to hie,
> I shall her goodly countenance espie,
> For there her goodly countenance I've seen,
> Set off with kerchief starch'd and pinners clean.
> Sometimes, like wax, she rolls the butter round,
> Or with the wooden lilly prints the pound.
> Whilome I've seen her skim the clouted cream,
> And press from spongy curds the milky stream.
> But now, alas! these ears shall hear no more
> The whining swine surround the dairy door,
> No more her care shall fill the hollow tray,
> To fat the guzzling hogs with floods of whey.
> Lament, ye swine, in grunting spend your grief,
> For you, like me, have lost your sole relief.   (55–68)

The "Proeme" contains a possibly unironic reference to the "plain, downright, hearty, cleanly folk" of the English countryside; and at times in the eclogues themselves it seems as if Gay is caught by his own delight in country customs and activities, and by nostalgia for his own boyhood in Devon; so that, in the act of mocking the idea of an Arcadia in contemporary England, he offers a half-truthful, half-idyllic representation of rural simplicity and felicity. One must not be tempted to read *The Shepherd's Week* sentimentally, even though many eighteenth-century critics succumbed to this temptation, but the ambiguous nature of Gay's pastorals appears clearly when they are contrasted with such straightforward burlesque or travesty as Swift's *Pastoral Dialogue*, "Dermot and Sheelah" (1729), and Gay's burlesque of Virgil's eclogue 4, *The Birth of the Squire* (1720), with its savage attack upon a boorish, lecherous, drunken, tyrannical landowner.

Johnson, in his *Life* of Gay, connects *The Shepherd's Week* with the Pope–Philips quarrel and assumes that Gay's intention was "to show, that if it be necessary to copy nature with minuteness, rural life must be exhibited such as grossness and ignorance have made it." "But," he continues,

the effect of reality and truth became conspicuous, even when the intention was to show them grovelling and degraded. These Pastorals became popular, and were read with delight as just representations of rural manners and occupations, by those who had no interest in the rivalry of the poets, nor knowledge of the critical dispute.

Allan Ramsay (1686–1758) was one such delighted reader. He wrote commendatory verses to Gay and joined the ranks of serious naturalizers with his eclogue in Scots vernacular *Patie and Roger* (1721), incorporated later into a pastoral comedy, *The Gentle Shepherd*. The setting of this eclogue is the Pentland Hills, but the matter is conventional pastoral love-complaint:

> I wish I cou'dna loo her—but in vain,
> I still maun dote, and thole [endure] her proud disdain....
> Flocks, wander where ye like, I dinna care
> I'll break my reed, and never whistle mair.[2]   (83–84, 95–96)

Ramsay's use of "Scotch Doric" prompted a succession of northern English poets to write dialect pastorals. Josiah Relph (1712–43), the son of a Cumberland "statesman," wrote three pastoral eclogues in the later 1720s or early 1730s (published 1747), and was the forerunner of a line of pastoralists and balladists writing in "Cumbrian Doric," Ewan Clark, Mark Lonsdale, John Stagg, and Robert Anderson; but only Relph avoids Ramsay's sentimentality and recaptures Gay's particular manner of half-sympathetic mockery.

By the 1730s and 1740s the "naturalized" eclogue in imitation of *The Shepherd's Week*, but without any burlesque intention, had become commonplace, and a tendency to naturalize without burlesque is everywhere apparent in forms of pastoral other than the eclogue. For instance, the fable or short verse tale, a common eighteenth-century form after the success of fable collections by La Fontaine and Gay, provides examples of particularized and sympathetic descriptions of rustics. In "The Contented Clown, a Tale" (*Gentleman's Magazine*, October 1739) there is a cottage interior:

> Five wooden Platters in a comely Row,
> With eke as many Beechen Spoons below;
> An Iron Pot stood open to the View,
> By which that he good Living kept you knew;
> On half one Side the antique Bed was plac'd,
> One whole Chair, and three broke, the other grac'd;
> All that you cou'd unnecessary call,
> Were some old tatter'd Ballads on the Wall.

This interior is possibly worked up from a hint in Swift's "Baucis and Philemon," but the poet displays a painterly zest for the concrete details of a poor small farmer's existence. The moral of his tale is unexceptionably "pastoral," for the contented clown does not envy his wealthy landlord.

A broadside ballad, "The Happy Clown," adapts more conventional pastoral and Horatian sentiments to its low subject,

> Like those in golden ages born,
> He labours gently to adorn
> His small paternal fields of corn,
> And on their product feeds;

But there is a fresh and perfect blend of observation and idyll in Ramsay's song,

> The lass of Peaty's Mill,
> So bonny, blyth, and gay,
> In spite of all my skill,
> Hath stole my heart away.
> When tedding of the day,
> Bare-headed on the green,
> Love'midst her locks did play,
> And wanton'd in her een.

Both those songs are in an anthology edited by Ramsay, *The Tea-Table Miscellany* (1724–37)[3] which was reprinted many times in the eighteenth century. It consists largely of pastoral songs, and testifies to the admirable lyrical art of a period which has sometimes absurdly been called an "Age of Prose."

Ramsay was a pioneer collector of old Scots songs and ballads, some of which he published in *Scots Songs* (1718–20) and *The Ever-Green* (1724), thus helping to widen the range of pastoral available for critical attention; and when John Langhorne in a late review (1762) of *The Ever-Green* declared that "Robene and Makyne" by the fifteenth-century poet Henryson was Theocritean,[4] he intended the highest praise. In the middle of the eighteenth century a revaluation of Theocritus is associated not only with the revival of interest in folk literature and early British poetry, but with that other "romantic" tendency, a so-called "return to nature." Theocritus is praised by Joseph Warton in the 1750s for realism, simplicity, "romantic rusticity," "lively pictures of the passions and of simple unadorned nature," and "rural, romantic wildness of thought, heightened by the Doric dialect": Theocritus "described what he saw and felt."[5] This may not be our reading of Theocritus today, but it was widely accepted in the later eighteenth century, and remained current for most of Wordsworth's lifetime.

Virgil was still the supreme ancient poet, but after Pope's *Pastorals* Virgil's influence was felt as much through the *Georgics* as the *Eclogues*. At a time when poets had generally abandoned epical ambitions the georgic was the highest available kind of nondramatic poetry, and the English poem that most fully achieved the grandeur and amplitude appropriate to this kind was *The Seasons* (1726–46) of James Thomson (1700–1748). The poem embraces several kinds of writing and not a few philosophical contradictions. The opening lines of "Autumn," for instance, see farming as the foundation of empire and a high level of material comfort for a nation, leading ultimately to such blessings as a refined textile technology, cities, the British Constitution, and world-wide commerce; but in the closing lines, modeled upon Virgil's "O fortunatos," farming is the nurse of simple virtue, and Thomson offers a vision of the innocence and joy of English country life, explicitly contrasted with city vice and misery. He claims

> This is the life which those who fret in guilt,
> And guilty cities never knew—the life,
> Led by primeval ages uncorrupt
> When angels dwelt, and God himself, with man![6]
>
> ("Autumn," ll. 1348–51)

That is, that contemporary Englishmen in their own countryside can recapture the primal innocence of the Golden Age or the Garden of Eden. Less extravagantly, in such a fine climactic passage as the description of hay-harvest and sheep-shearing in "Summer" (352–431) Thomson offers a characteristic blend of idyll and observation, that might be described as "soft realism."

Christopher Smart (1722–71) in *The Hop-Garden, a Georgic* (1752) paints a Kentish landscape with "blest denizens" "in fair Madum's vale / Imparadis'd" (bk. 1, l. 38). In another georgic, *Agriculture* (1753) by Robert Dodsley (1703–64), cottages are "scenes of innocence and calm delight" (bk. 1, l. 321), while the description of a hiring fair includes a series of rural sketches where idealization culminates in the portrait of young Patty the milkmaid, as beautiful "As an Arcadian nymph" in whose eyes "Young sensibility began to play with innocence" (bk. 1, l. 139). This sentimentalizing of rural society is completed when Patty is wooed and won by a squire, Thyrsis, in an episode modeled upon the Lavinia and Palemon tale in Thomson's *The Seasons*.

For Dodsley, a hiring-fair is the "feast of willing servitude" (*Agriculture*, bk. 1, l. 106); but a less abstract notion of work is offered by that farm-laborer-turned-poet, Stephen Duck (1705–56). In "The Thresher's Labour" (*Poems on Several Subjects*, 1730) when he struggles free from misplaced metaphor and creaking mythology, he

can recount some of the facts of rural life and labor quite effectively
in the manner characteristic of his class—grumpy, yet fatalistic:

> No fountains murmur here, no Lambkins play,
> No Linnets warble, and no Fields look gay;
> 'Tis all a gloomy, melancholy Scene,
> Fit only to provoke the Muse's Spleen.
> When sooty Pease we thresh, you scarce can know
> Our native Colour, as from Work we go:
> The Sweat, the Dust, and suffocating Smoke,
> Make us so much like Ethiopians look,
> We scare our Wives, when Ev'ning brings us home;
> And frighted Infants think the Bugbear come.
> Week after Week, we this dull Task pursue,
> Unless when winn'wing Days produce a new;
> A new, indeed, but frequently a worse!
> The threshal yields but to the Master's Curse.
> He counts the Bushels, counts how much a day;
> Then swears we've idled half our Time away.   (58–73)

With its repetition of "we," this is almost the authentic "voice from
below." Duck was duly hailed by a group of kindly gentlemen as
an embodiment of the "natural genius" that Addison had postulated
in *Spectator*, no. 160 (1711), but after he was summoned from the
laborer's cottage to take tea with Queen Caroline, and ultimately
to become her highness's pet at Kew, he turned to very conventional
sub-Virgilian pastoral. His example, and an ever-intensifying search
by eighteenth-century literati for examples of "natural genius," encouraged other "heaven-taught" laboring men and women to come
forward as versifiers.[7] Not only was it becoming axiomatic that the
poor deserved a song, but the poor were determined to sing it.
  Thomas Gray (1716–71) mused upon the hypothetical "natural
genius," the laborer poet, in his *Elegy written in a Country Church-
Yard* (1751):

> Perhaps in this neglected spot is laid
> Some heart once pregnant with celestial fire,
> Hands, that the rod of empire might have sway'd,
> Or wak'd to extasy the living lyre.

Gray's *Elegy* draws a commonplace pastoral contrast between the useful toil of the villagers and the pomp of power. There is a hint of rural disharmony in the reference to the "little tyrant of his fields" withstood by the village Hampden or, in the Eton College manuscript, "Cato"; but the final injunction "submit to Fate" reinforces the tone and imagery of the poem in anaesthetizing any potential social protest. Gray's poem was the origin of a regular subgenre of "pauper elegies." Two of the most frequently anthologized pieces in this kind are W. H. Roberts's *The Poor Man's Prayer* "by Simon Hedge" (1766), and *The Beggar's Petition* (1769) by Thomas Moss, which arouse sympathy for the hardships of evicted small farmers. Present misery is contrasted with a recent past in which these rustics led the conventionally idyllic existence of the "happy husbandman."

Extended treatments of this pathetic theme of rural expropriation are to be found in Laurence Whyte's long descriptive piece "The Parting Cup" in *Poems on Various Subjects* (1740), and "Snaith Marsh, a Yorkshire Pastoral" by "Ophelia" (*Gentleman's Magazine*, March 1754). The first is chiefly of interest because Goldsmith probably knew it and its author, and possibly derived suggestions from it for *The Deserted Village*. The second retains the conventional pastoral eclogue form and some of its conventional subject matter along with altogether "modern" matter. Its author uneasily combines authentic dialect and poetic diction in recounting both the amorous pains and the more real moral and material sufferings of a cottager whose livelihood and matrimonial hopes disappear at one blow with the enclosure of a common, which happens to be an actual common in South Yorkshire:

> Snaith Marsh, our whole Town's Pride, the poor Man's Bread,
> Where, tho' no Rent he paid, his Cattle fed,
> Fed on the sweetest Grass which here rife grew,
> Common to all, nor Fence, nor Landmark knew,
> Whose flowery Turf no crooked Share had raz'd,
> Nor wide destroying Scythe its Green effac'd.
> But now, ah! now, it stoops, sad seet I ween,
> In mony a Row, with Rails suspended 'tween.

Among eighteenth-century poems that set pastoral idyll against facts of social and economic upheaval in the countryside *The Deserted*

Village (1770) stands supreme. Goldsmith first treated the subject of deserted villages in his essay "The Revolution in Low Life" (1762), with a detailed account of an emparking enclosure which, he claimed, occurred the previous summer about fifty miles from London.[8] Inhabitants of nearly a hundred houses were evicted because "a Merchant of immense fortune in London, who had lately purchased the estate on which they lived, intended to lay the whole out in a seat of pleasure for himself."[9] In *The Traveller* (1764) he made a more generalized protest: "Have we not seen at pleasure's lordly call, / The smiling long-frequented village fall?" (405–6). Finally, in his account of the desertion of Auburn, Goldsmith established the myth of rural catastrophe in its familiar form. The myth rests upon the clear fact that villages were being destroyed to make way for rich men's pleasure grounds. Castle Howard, Cirencester Park, Crichel, Harewood, Holkham, Houghton, Kedleston, Mereworth, Milton Abbas, Normanton, Nuneham Courtenay, Shottesbrooke, Stowe, and Wimpole were among the gardens that ate up villages in the eighteenth century. These landscape gardens sought to give physical shape to great landowners' conceptions—derived from classical pastoral direct, or at one remove through the paintings of Claude Lorraine—of Arcadia, the Vale of Tempe, the Golden Age. But for Goldsmith the laying out of such pleasure grounds signaled the destruction of another Arcadia or Golden Age, the joy and virtue and independence of a community of happy husbandmen.

The desertion of Auburn is Goldsmith's occasion for an attack upon "luxury" and the excessive power of trading interests, and so the poem is a tract for the times, but Burke was correct in describing it as a pastoral, whose images "beat all Pope and Philips and Spenser too in my opinion, that is in the Pastoral."[10] The setting is in some respects a workaday English village:

> The sheltered cot, the cultivated farm,
> The never failing brook, the busy mill,
> The decent church that topt the neighbouring hill,
> The hawthorn bush, with seats beneath the shade.   (10–13)

but it shares some features of the idyllic landscapes of classical pastoral: "The cooling brook, the grassy vested green, / The breezy covert of the warbling grove" (360–61). Before its destruction,

Auburn is a "sweet smiling village" (35, cf. 1, 75, 123, 337); Goldsmith echoes the opening verses of Theocritus's first idyll in "Sweet was the sound when oft at evening's close, / Up yonder hill the village murmur rose" (113–14). In Theocritus, sweet sounds are the mutually responsive music of shepherds, pine grove, and stream, whereas in Goldsmith the activity of men, women, children, and farm animals, create "the sounds of population" (125), which "in sweet confusion sought the shade, / And filled each pause the nightingale had made" (123–24). Among them, the "mingling notes" of "The swain responsive as the milk-maid sung" (116–17) call to mind conventional pastoral dialogue.

As this poem is a pastoral elegy upon a departed community, it is appropriate that external nature should mourn:

> No more thy glassy brook reflects the day,
> But choaked with sedges, works its weedy way.
> Along thy glades, a solitary guest.
> The hollow sounding bittern guards its nest;
> Amidst thy desert walks the lapwing flies,
> And tires their ecchoes with unvaried cries.
> Sunk are thy bowers in shapeless ruin all,
> And the long grass o'ertops the mouldering wall.   (41–48)

The scene is suffused with the pastoral singer's own feelings: "Remembrance wakes with all her busy train, / Swells at my breast, and turns the past to pain" (82–83). This couplet introduces a "retirement" passage (lines 82–112) where the subjective element becomes insistent, and rises to an emotional climax with the image of the poet as a hunted hare; for the singer sees not only the object of his sorrow but himself in a suitable attitude before it. He is something of the sentimentalist who withdraws into himself to contemplate his own feelings, but he also looks outward in a purposeful manner. The main theme of the poem is introduced with the words:

> Ye friends to truth, ye statesmen who survey
> The rich man's joys encrease, the poor's decay,
> 'Tis yours to judge, how wide the limits stand
> Between a splendid and an happy land.   (265–68)

The pastoral theme of virtue in humble rural life is proclaimed in references to the villagers collectively and elaborated in sketches of individuals, one of which, the solitary, dispossessed, sad matron, is a stock character of humanitarian literature, though she may also be that common enough figure—the poor decrepit man or woman housed by a depopulating landlord in order to prevent his being obliged to pay toward the support of the poor in the next parish. The contrasts that provide an intellectual framework for the poem are those of the pastoral: nature against art, country against city, and frugality against luxury. Goldsmith's conception of a sturdy, free peasantry, living virtuously in humble mediocrity, is the regular pastoral-georgic-natural-man ideal. In his prefatory letter to Reynolds he professes himself an "ancient," and his denunciation of the enormous increase in foreign trade, with concentration of excessive wealth and power in too few hands and a consequent threat to the liberties of the nation, is made in the light of the ideal of simple, virtuous, republican Rome. The famous claim "A time there was, ere England's griefs began, / When every rood of ground maintained its man," has its counterpart in contemporary political pamphlets on enclosures and engrossing, but Goldsmith is not offering a definite program of agrarian reform. The poem's dominant mood is pathos, certainly not radical zeal; nevertheless, Goldsmith combines the contemporary fact of rural oppression—taking the morally simple case of an emparking enclosure, indefensible on economic as well as on moral grounds—with an appealing, idealistic, yet plausible retrospective peasant Arcadia that would serve the cause of political radicalism in the 1790s.

Radical feeling, though, is not at all evident in the first wave of "pauper poetry" that followed *The Deserted Village.* John Robinson of Norwich, in *The Village Oppress'd* (1771), recalls times which "memory well can trace" when "The harmless peasants were a happy race," complains of the avarice, pride and luxury which "Have farm to farm annex'd, and field to field," and denounces the cit who parades his wealth by extending his park over peasants' holdings, and by bringing to the countryside all the modish vices of the town. John Scott (1730–83) has a Deserted Village situation in "Armyn," one of *Four Moral Eclogues* (1778), but avoids any radical implications of protest most circumspectly. He presents the evicted shepherd Albino lamenting that, where he once saw a beautiful, varied, and animated landscape of fields and windmills and "pleasant village scenes," a proud lord now,

> in lonely grandeur reigns;
> His wide-spread park a waste of verdure lies,
> And his vast villa's glittering roofs arise.

The sneering *v* of verdure, which is paradoxically conjoined with "waste," and of the paradoxical "vast villa," though unsubtle, has some abusive force. But Albino continues:

> For me, hard fate! But say, shall I complain?
> These limbs yet active life's support obtain.
> Let us, or good or evil as we share,
> That thankful prize, and this with patience bear.

Floundering in a drivel of syntactical inversions Scott preaches resignation to the poor.

The contribution of *The Deserted Village* to radical thought was delayed until the 1790s, but the poem had an immediate effect in further popularizing humanitarian, half-patronizing sketches of rustic characters.[11] Some particularly vivid and sympathetically observed examples of such characters may be found in *The Farmer's Ingle* (1773) by Robert Fergusson (1750–74) who belongs to the Shenstone-Goldsmith pastoral line, while drawing upon a Scots vernacular tradition reanimated by Ramsay. He writes of the usual "happy husbandman" theme, but his language, unlike that of most English pastoralists, is to a great extent the language of the society he describes. William Cowper's pictures of the poor in *The Task* (1785) are more individualized and "picturesque" than Goldsmith's, a point which may be demonstrated by comparing, say, Cowper's Crazy Kate (bk. 1, ll. 534–66) and Goldsmith's sad matron (129–36). Cowper takes a kindly interest in the deserving poor as objects for patronage, he recognizes the hardships of the country laborer's life, but finds many of the undeserving poor to condemn (bk. 4, ll. 333–512). His paraphrase of Varro, "God made the country, man made the town," and his lamentations over the evil influence of the town in disturbing rural peace and virtue,

> The town has ting'd the country; and the stain
> Appears a spot upon a vestal's robe,
> The worse for what it soils (bk. 4, ll. 532-34)[12]

rest upon idyllic assumptions, even though, in the same breath, he
mildly satirizes pastoral convention:

> those golden times,
> And those Arcadian scenes, that Maro sings.
> ... innocence, it seems,
> From courts dismiss'd, found shelter in the groves....
> Vain wish! Those days were never: airy dreams
> Sat for the picture; and the poet's hand,
> Imparting substance to an empty shade,
> Imposed a gay delirium for a truth. (bk. 4, ll. 514-28)

In George Crabbe satire against conventional pastoral is not crossed
by sentimental contradictions, for *The Village* (1783) was composed
under Burke's eye and received Johnson's approval. Lines improved
by Johnson's firm hand emphatically repudiate idyllic convention:

> On Mincio's banks, in Caesar's bounteous reign,
> If Tityrus found the Golden Age again,
> Must sleepy bards the flattering dream prolong,
> Mechanic echoes of the Mantuan song?
> From Truth and Nature shall we widely stray,
> Where Virgil, not where Fancy, leads the way.[13]
>   (bk. 1, ll. 15-20)

Johnson demands that a poet should follow "Fancy" (i.e., imagination), not Virgil, but in Crabbe's original text the last line of this
passage reads, "Where Fancy leads, or Virgil led the way," asserting
that neither imagination nor Virgil are sure guides to "Truth and
Nature." Crabbe calls for a poetry of direct, unclouded observation.
His real "picture of the poor" is addressed to sentimental idealists
of his own day:

> Go, then! and see them rising with the sun,
> Through a long course of daily toil to run....

See them alternate suns and showers engage,
And hoard up aches and anguish for their age.
(bk. 1, ll. 142–49)

Crabbe's swains are not healthy and happy; nor are they innocent, for they include bribable electors, and (as a caustic variety of piscatorial eclogue) fishermen and wreckers:

Here, wand'ring long, amid these frowning fields,
I sought the simple life that Nature yields;
Rapine and Wrong and Fear usurp'd her place,
And a bold, artful, surly, savage race.
Who, only skill'd to take the finny tribe,
The yearly dinner, or septennial bribe,
Wait on the shore, and, as the waves run high,
On the tost vessel bend their eager eye. (bk. 1, ll. 109–16)

Crabbe vigorously denies benevolent assumptions about the virtuous nature of "natural man," and directs his satire as much against modern naturalized, humanitarian pastoral, as against dreamy imitations of Virgil, but the stated theme of the poem (announced at bk. 2, ll. 87–106) is the equality of human conditions. The climax is a lengthy elegy on Lord Robert Manners, when Crabbe asks the poor to consider the pains and dangers of his lordship's life and "let your murmurs cease, / Think, think of him, and take your lot in peace." This closely follows a scene where a lecherous justice of the peace recites the law to a village strumpet; and the awkward transition—the moral clashing of gears—with which Crabbe reestablishes a beautiful relationship between rich and poor ("the essential trick of the old pastoral," as Empson wrote) has an effect not unlike the appalling conclusion of Scott's moral eclogue, "Armyn," quoted above. "Shall I dare?" asked Crabbe, but his daring did not extend to questioning the social order any more than, or even as much as, Goldsmith had done. Where Crabbe does advance beyond earlier pastoral is in developing, out of the "low descriptions"—satirical, sentimental or neutral—found in poets as various as Swift, Gay, Duck, Shenstone, and the anonymous magazine and miscellany sketchers of the "Contented Clown," the "Parish Clerk," and their like, that technique of "Dutch painting" which his first reviewers saw as his distinctive gift. Crabbe might declare "Fled are those times, if e'er such times were seen, / When rustic poets prais'd their native green"; but since the discovery in 1730 of Stephen Duck, whom Crabbe himself mentions (*The Village*, bk. 1, l. 27), hardly a year had passed without some peasant poet being brought forward and hailed as a "natural genius." Thus there was a calculated appeal to the literati on the title page of Robert Burns's Kilmarnock volume of 1786, proclaiming its author as "The Simple Bard, unbroke by rules of Art." Far from being artless Burns was a careful craftsman working consciously in the English and Scots eighteenth-century traditions, but he was also in Sir Walter Scott's words, "*the douce guidman* who held his own plough." So he avoids sentimentality and farce alike in treating subjects which would probably tend one way or the other in the hands of writers not intimately involved in farming. In "The Auld Farmer's New-Year Morning Salutation to his Auld Mare Maggie," for instance, he displays respect and affection for his plough horse as working companion and capital asset, while he displays the real joys of the husbandman and compensation for hours of back-breaking labor—pride in one's craft and the satisfaction of making good bargains. In "The Twa Dogs" the ploughman's dog shows that the peasant contrives to be happy despite insecurity and the oppressions of an absentee landlord and his proud and greedy factor. The reply of the gentleman's dog indicates that the great are more miserable than the poor: the conclusion of the poem, however, is not the old pastoral moral of the superior joy and virtue of the husbandman's life, but a doggy and democratic headshake over the paradoxes of human nature.

The poet hailed as an English Burns was that mild-mannered, humble rustic, the once-famous Robert Bloomfield, whose *The Farmer's Boy* (1800) is a rhymed imitation of Thomson's *The Seasons*, but with descriptions localized in Suffolk. Most of Bloomfield's poem is idyllic in tone, but in the last hundred lines of "Summer" he introduces a complaint about the polarization of rural society that had already been heard in much humanitarian verse, and even in Crabbe's *The Village*. He touches on the sweet Auburn myth of an era of small, equal, independent farmers with their new-fangled ways of aping the gentry, adding as footnote a description of the simplicity and social equality of the Tahitians. Nothing could more

artlessly show how eighteenth-century nostalgic primitivism was all
of a piece—peasants of one's own youth and South Sea islanders
enjoyed or enjoy the same Golden Age.

There is a hint of unspoiled Auburn in the domestic comforts and
parlor splendors among peasant joys whose loss is lamented in
Southey's "Humphrey and William," one of four *Botany-bay Eclogues*
written in 1794. Southey's formal arrangement of these eclogues—
setting the action of each in a different hour, morning, noon, evening,
night—follows Pope, but his subject matter is uncompromisingly
"modern"; for his characters are convicts, victims of unjust social and
penal systems. The subjects of those four eclogues—poverty and oppression, guilt and sorrow, change in the countryside and war—recur
in Southey's *English Eclogues* written between 1797 and 1803, and
the sober pathos of one of these, "The Ruined Cottage," owes more
than a hint to Wordsworth who, when Southey first met him in
1795, was already at work on his own poem of the same title.

Chapter Eleven

Wordsworth

At the time he met Southey, Wordsworth's verse was full of socially oppressed figures and outcasts. In his "Salisbury Plain" poem, begun about 1791, some stanzas of which were published in *Lyrical Ballads* (1798) under the title of "The Female Vagrant," he takes commonplace characters and themes of humanitarian verse of the later eighteenth century: beggar woman, gypsies, discharged sailor, smallholder forced by poverty to enlist as a soldier, horrors of war, and evil consequences of the engrossing of farms. The female vagrant's existence was as idyllic as life in unspoiled Auburn until nearby there rose the "mansion proud" of an engrossing landlord. She is the successor of Goldsmith's "widowed solitary thing" and has a counterpart in Cowper's Crazy Kate, but where those characters are observed picturesquely she is conceived dramatically. Even so, Wordsworth was dissatisfied and thought "The Female Vagrant" was "merely descriptive," though the force of this charge can only be appreciated if this poem is compared with "The Ruined Cottage" or "Michael."

"The Ruined Cottage" (written 1797; expanded and revised to constitute book 1 of *The Excursion*, 1814) is the story of an ordinary woman, Margaret, whose husband is compelled by economic depression in the 1780s to enlist as a soldier and is never heard of again, though his "Wife and Widow," through nine tedious years of solitude and destitution, never gives up hope of his return. Her sufferings and death, as narrated to the poet by an aged pedlar, are reflected in a progressive decay of garden and cottage. The ruined cottage and weed-choked garden in which the poet listens to the story represent the final stage of the story itself, and continuously suggest a contrast between past and present, much as the decayed cottages of *The Deserted Village* do. Here, as in ruined Auburn, "the long grass o'ertops the mouldering wall," but the pedlar discovers in that image of desolation,

> Those weeds, and the high spear-grass on that wall,
> By mist and silent rain-drops silver'd o'er,
> . . . an image of tranquility.[1] (*The Excursion*, bk. 1, ll. 943–46)

Correspondingly, in nature's reasserting its hold upon the once-cultivated garden, the poet traces

> That secret spirit of humanity
> Which, 'mid the calm oblivious tendencies
> Of nature, 'mid her plants, and weeds, and flowers,
> And silent overgrowings, still survived. (927–30)

For the seeing eye this particular landscape is given permanent significance by its relationship with Margaret's sufferings, and for the meditative mind the dead Margaret is assimilated into the calm of external nature in a consoling way. "The Ruined Cottage" is a pastoral elegy which is historically accurate, in that it is founded even more surely than *The Deserted Village* on contemporary social and economic realities, but which is also psychologically true. It is a meditation upon the universal mystery of suffering in which the pastoral "pathetic fallacy" of a bond between man and nature is seen as a function of the projective imagination, and to that degree not fallacious:

> The Poets, in their elegies and songs
> Lamenting the departed, call the groves,
> They call upon the hills and streams to mourn,
> And senseless rocks; nor idly; for they speak,
> In these their invocations, with a voice
> Obedient to the strong creative power
> Of human passion. Sympathies there are
> More tranquil, yet perhaps of kindred birth,
> That steal upon the meditative mind,
> And grow with thought. (475–84)

Such sympathies, by which the mind of man is wedded to this goodly universe, are a major theme, perhaps *the* major theme, of the great

body of Wordsworth's poetry; so, in a sense, all his most significant
work is pastoral, even though that term appears in the titles of very
few of his poems.[2]
     The most notable of these is "Michael, a Pastoral Poem" (*Lyrical
Ballads*, 1800), which takes the life of a real shepherd as its subject
and is cast in conventional eclogue form, inasmuch as the narrative
is framed by an introduction (1–39) in which the poet declares his
purpose in telling so homely and rude a "domestic" tale,

> For the delight of a few natural hearts;
> And, with yet fonder feeling, for the sake
> Of youthful Poets, who among these hills
> Will be my second self when I am gone.   (36–39)

Even more obviously than Theocritus's idyll 7, "Michael" is a poetic
manifesto: Wordsworth, a modern Lycidas, invites the Simichidases
of the nineteenth century to follow him in opposition to those contemporary romantic tendencies in stories that were "enriched with
strange events" (19). An episode originally intended for "Michael"
is no less appropriately incorporated into Wordsworth's narrative of
the development of his own sensibility and imagination, *The Prelude*,
where this "true pastoral" (bk. 8, ll. 211–310, 1805 version) is contrasted with artificial pastoral. This episode has a roll call (229–43)
of local place names unparalleled elsewhere in Wordsworth, but the
published "Michael" is just as surely a local poem, set firmly in that
society described in Wordsworth's *A Guide through the District of
the Lakes*—a society which "exhibited a perfect equality, a community
of shepherds and agriculturalists, proprietors, for the most part, of
the lands which they occupied and cultivated" (second section, 1835
ed.). Wordsworth always idealizes this society, and when he describes
it in verse, significantly he finds it easy to slip into the attitudes and
even the phrases of Virgil's *Georgics*:

> Where kindred independence of estate
> Is prevalent, where he who tills the field,
> He, happy Man! is Master of the field,
> And treads the mountains which his Fathers trod.
>   ("Home at Grasmere," ll. 380–83)

In "Michael" that ancient pastoral theme of the deeply felt bond between man and external nature is no sentimental fiction. Michael's past emotional life is recorded in the features of the land which he owns and works, and so when he sees the spot where he once rescued a sheep the mechanism of affective memory is set in motion, reinforced, credibly enough, by economic motives:

> And grossly that man errs, who should suppose
> That the green valleys, and the streams and rocks,
> Were things indifferent to the Shepherd's thought.
> Fields, where with cheerful spirits he had breathed
> The common air; hills, which with vigorous step
> He had so often climbed; which had impressed
> So many incidents upon his mind
> Of hardship, skill or courage, joy or fear;
> Which, like a book, preserved the memory
> Of the dumb animals, whom he had saved,
> Had fed or sheltered, linking to such acts
> The certainty of honourable gain;
> Those fields, those hills—what could they less? had laid
> Strong hold on his affections, were to him
> A pleasurable feeling of blind love,
> The pleasure which there is in life itself.   (62–77)

The bond between peasant and land is such that the sad history is not completed until a ploughshare has been through the ground where Michael's cottage once stood. The theme of rural expropriation running through pastoral from Virgil's eclogue 1 to *The Deserted Village* finds a more commonplace, more human, and yet more grandly tragic expression.

As Goldsmith saw *The Deserted Village*, so Wordsworth saw "Michael" as a political weapon. In a letter dated 14 January 1801 he drew the attention of Charles James Fox to his poem, and to another pastoral in the 1800 volume, "The Brothers," declaring:

I have attempted to draw a picture of the domestic affections as I know they exist amongst a class of men who are now almost confined to the North of England. They are small independent proprietors of land here called statesmen, men of respectable education who daily labour on their own little properties. The domestic affections will always be strong amongst men who live in a country not crowded with population, if these men are placed above poverty. But if they are proprietors of small estates, which have descended to them from their ancestors, the power which these affections will acquire amongst such men is inconceivable by those who have only had an opportunity of observing hired labourers, farmers, and the manufacturing Poor. Their little tract of land serves as a kind of permanent rallying point for their domestic feelings, as a tablet upon which they are written which makes them objects of memory in a thousand instances when they would otherwise be forgotten. It is a fountain fitted to the nature of social man from which supplies of affection, as pure as his heart was intended for, are daily drawn. This class of men is rapidly disappearing. You, Sir, have a consciousness, upon which every good man will congratulate you, that the whole of your public conduct has in one way or other been directed to the preservation of this class of men, and those who hold similar situations.

Wordsworth's letter to Fox expresses something closely akin to the conservatism of Virgil's *Georgics*. The small farmer's attachment to his own soil was, in Wordsworth's view, the foundation of virtue and "the tap root of the tree of Patriotism." In his later years the author of "Michael" was to oppose the Reform Act of 1832 because it gave the franchise to men who had no landed property, and therefore could not, in the nature of things, be true patriots. This is an attitude that most eighteenth-century writers would have understood and shared.

The character of Michael combines traces of the usual happy husbandman ideal of independence, hardihood, and virtue, with hints of a biblical patriarch, as when he makes a covenant with his son; but he is a far more credibly motivated and far more truly human figure than any other shepherd of eighteenth-century pastoral. Wordsworth attributes to him something of the natural grandeur and sublimity of the hills which are his home; the blank verse draws the poem, for all its simple diction and syntax, toward the sublime mood. Nevertheless "Michael" amply bears out the claim in the "Advertisement" to *Lyrical Ballads* that Wordsworth's poems would afford "a natural delineation of human passions, human characters, and human incidents." The poem forms a most effective reply to Johnson's charge in *Rambler*, no. 35, that a man will not "after the perusal of thousands [of pastorals] find his knowledge enlarged with a single view of nature not produced before, or his imagination amused with any new application of those views to moral purposes." In this and other Wordsworth poems the pastoral picturesque/humanitarian stage-army of virtuous peasants and peasants' children corrupted in the city, of beggars, discharged soldiers and the rest, marches around once again, but suddenly we are involved in a deep drama of "man, the heart of man, and human life."

Wordsworth's achievement was to attach a deeper significance to the pastoral occupation and setting in literature. Michael's life is more decent and worthy than a city dweller's could be because it has an organic wholeness embracing work, morality, and aesthetic experience. The everyday life of a Lakeland shepherd is a way of feeling and knowing. In *The Prelude* Wordsworth gave meaning to Gray's rhetorical flourish about some "mute inglorious Milton":

> There are among the walks of homely life
> Still higher, men for contemplation framed,
> Shy, and unpractis'd in the strife of phrase;
> Meek men, whose very souls perhaps would sink
> Beneath them, summon'd to such intercourse:
> Theirs is the language of the heavens, the power,
> The thought, the image, and the silent joy:
> Words are but under-agents in their souls.[3]
>
> (bk. 12, ll, 265–72)

The forms of nature have according to Wordsworth's animistic belief, a moral and spiritual life, and Lakeland shepherds thus are blessed:

> them the morning light
> Loves, as it glistens on the silent rocks,
> And them the silent rocks, which now from high
> Look down upon them; the reposing clouds,
> The lurking brooks from their invisible haunts;
> And Old Helvellyn....
> And the blue sky that roofs their calm abode.
>
> (bk. 8, ll. 55–61)

This calm abode, we are told in a series of comparisons (119–43) echoing Milton's account of the Garden of Eden, is lovelier than any

fabled paradise; but motifs of golden-age pastoral are combined with
georgic in Wordsworth's description:

> a district on all sides
> The fragrance breathing of humanity,
> Man free, man working for himself, with choice
> Of time, and place, and object; by his wants,
> His comforts, native occupations, cares,
> Conducted on to individual ends
> Or social, and still followed by a train
> Unwooed, unthought-of even—simplicity,
> And beauty, and inevitable grace.   (150–58)

Like Virgil's happy husbandman and like Michael, these independent
shepherd-proprietors are blessed without thinking of their blessings.

Wordsworth's sober, thoughtful, particularized, and credible pastoral is accompanied by an expected repudiation of conventional pastoral. The reader is not surprised to learn that Lakeland shepherds
do not resemble those of Arcadia, or of Spenser and Shakespeare
(183–91, 312–24); but Wordsworth insists that neither are they
associated with genuine English folk-memories of the rural delights
of Merry England, such as May-Day celebrations (191–205), nor
do they resemble real, leisured, piping shepherds such as he had observed for himself from the walls of Goslar in Germany (324–53).
The pastoral landscape of Goslar is one "where Fancy might run
wild" (326), and Wordsworth, like Crabbe, will not be led astray
by Fancy any more than by Virgil; nevertheless, the Wordsworthian
shepherd, in his "severe and unadorned" life, could take on a near-
supernatural magnificence:

> A rambling schoolboy, thus
> Have I beheld him, without knowing why
> Have felt his presence in his own domain,
> As of a lord and master, or a power,
> Or genius, under Nature, under God,
> Presiding. . . .
> His form hath flashed upon me, glorified
> By the deep radiance of the setting sun:
> Or him I have descried in distant sky,

A solitary object and sublime,
Above all height! like an aerial cross,
As it is stationed on some spiry rock
Of the Chartreuse, for worship.   (390–95, 404–10)

Despite his repudiation of conventional pastoral, Wordsworth still "loved / To dream of Sicily," as he declares at the end of book 10 of *The Prelude* in the 1805 version (book 11 in 1850), addressing Coleridge who was traveling in the Mediterranean. In this address Wordsworth recalls the song of Lycidas in Theocritus's idyll 7 which told how the goatherd-singer Comatas was shut in a chest by his tyrannical lord and left to starve, but, month after month, was fed by bees with honey from the fields, "Because the goatherd, blessed man! had lips / Wet with the Muse's nectar" (1027–28). Lycidas wishes that Comatas was with him now in some idyllic landscape, piping to their goats. Reference in *The Prelude* to this famous pastoral allegory of the divine power of poetry is itself a kind of bucolic masquerade, a brotherly tribute from Wordsworth–Lycidas, the true rural poet, to Coleridge–Comatas, the divine singer who "on honey-dew hath fed," but Wordsworth's recognition of the affinity between Theocritus and himself usually takes the more predictable form of a tribute to the Alexandrian poet's simplicity and truth to nature. In a letter to Coleridge, 27 February 1799, he writes: "read Theocritus in Ayrshire or Merionethshire and you will find perpetual occasions to recollect what you see daily in Ayrshire or Merionethshire, read Congreve, Vanbrugh and Farquhar in London and though not a century is elapsed since they were alive and merry, you will meet with whole pages that are uninteresting and incomprehensible." In a letter of 20 September 1824 he slyly bears out the accuracy of this generalization when he writes of milkmaids in North Wales: "How cheerful and happy they appeared! and not a little inclined to joke after the manner of the pastoral persons in Theocritus."

For his own verse Wordsworth sought the quality of permanence which he found in Theocritus. In the preface to *Lyrical Ballads*, 1802, he explains that for the subjects of his poems,

Low and rustic life was generally chosen because in that situation the essential passions of the heart find a better soil in which they can attain

their maturity, are less under restraint, and speak a plainer and more
emphatic language; because in that situation our elementary feelings
exist in a state of greater simplicity and consequently may be more accu-
rately contemplated and more forcibly communicated; because the manners of rural life germinate from those elementary feelings; and from
the necessary character of rural occupations are more easily comprehended;
and are more durable; and lastly, because in that situation the passions
of men are incorporated with the beautiful and permanent forms of
nature.

Wordsworth completes the eighteenth-century naturalization of pastoral, and, in his union of passion, simplicity, and truth, fully realizes
the idea of "romantic rusticity" which eighteenth-century critics recog-
nized in Theocritus. "The golden past and the pleasant place become a personal time and a personal landscape and yet retain the
equivalent of mythic dimensions. "Paradise, and grove / Elysian For-
tunate fields" need no longer be sought in ancient, fictional localities;
they are "the simple produce of the common day."[4] Pastoral does not
end with Wordsworth. Postromantic individualism in poets as various as Clare, Barnes, Hardy, Houseman, Shelley, Keats, Arnold,
Yeats, Tennyson, and Clough—not to mention their successors in the
twentieth century—created many more versions of pastoral poetry
than were known before the nineteenth century, but they do not
form part of that coherent pastoral tradition which descends unbroken,
albeit with intermittent vigour, from Theocritus and Virgil to the
late eighteenth century. Wordsworth on occasions saw himself as belonging to a living Theocritean tradition; but, more than any other
pastoral poet discussed in my book, he transcends that tradition. As
F. W. Bateson has shown, Wordsworth is, "with Blake, the first
specifically modern English poet."[5] Wordsworth's predecessors, however they may have sentimentalized, or socialized, or satirized, or
otherwise reshaped specific literary traditions, shared a belief in the
overall validity of the inherited literary tradition: "Poems like 'The
Idiot Boy,' 'We are Seven' and *Peter Bell* are not merely outside the
literary tradition—Blake's poems are outside it too—they are written
in a deliberate defiance of it."[6] In bringing about a revolution against
the literary-traditional element in poetry Wordsworth enormously
expanded the boundaries of art. He is the first great modern experi-
mental poet, nowhere more so than in *The Prelude* where a world

of new experience is made available for his successors; and with him begins the modern movement of entire self-expression as art and of improvisation as art. As I have said, there is pastoral poetry of many kinds in the nineteenth and twentieth centuries, some of it echoing the work of Theocritus and Virgil from which arose the tradition that lives transformed in some of Wordsworth's poems; but the revolutionary achievement of Wordsworth was to shatter the continuity of that literary tradition, and indeed to make the tradition altogether less relevant to the business of a poet. Therefore it is appropriate that an historical study of Theocritean–Virgilian pastoral in England should end with Wordsworth.

Chapter Twelve

Epilogue

Whether or not Theocritus was as simple as Wordsworth and many earlier English critics argued, his pastorals were the source of a varied, rich, and complex tradition. They established the shape and scope of a lyric-dramatic form in which, usually, a song or songs are set within a narrative or descriptive and reflective framework. They provided the outlines of a particular and distinctive setting for an age-old vision of happy, rural life, as contrasted with a complex, hectic, and miserable existence in court and city. The sweet tranquility of a pleasant landscape or the richness of a harvest feast correspond with serenity in man's heart and mind, to create an overall mood of stability, composure, and delight. This mood can be disturbed only by the pains of love, but even the bitterness and frustration of unrequited love is sweetly resolved in the herdsman's song. Some of these herdsmen—Corydon and Battus, for instance—represent simple, gross human nature, as observed patronizingly by the city poet, though, as the pastoral tradition developed in the Renaissance, it was found that rustic innocence and simplicity could be employed as sophisticated weapons against the vices of court and city. Other herdsmen in Theocritus, however, are figures of imaginative power and authority. Polyphemus, the fearsome monster of Homeric epic now humanized as the very type of passionate shepherd, finds healing in "the medicine of the Muses," and, by making in song an outlet for his feelings, discovers a psychology of art. Daphnis is a figure into whom pastoral tradition easily assimilates the vegetation spirit, Adonis; and in the sympathetic mourning of beasts and vegetation at a shepherd-singer's death—a mourning which magnifies yet calms sorrow—the natural world is mysteriously linked with human circumstances and feelings.

134

Simichidas is perhaps the shepherd-type with greatest authority of all, because he represents the poet himself.

In the songs of his various herdsmen and their settings, Theocritus defines the themes of most later pastoral: love, nature, and art. These, certainly, are Virgil's themes, but in his eclogues they are related to the painful complexities of social life. The tone is graver, whether in the love-melancholy of Gallus, or the misery of the expropriations alluded to in eclogues 1 and 9, giving rise to Moeris's reflection, "Time bears all away." Pastoral is brought into history and raised to philosophical status, so that, by comparison, the idylls of Theocritus appear lacking in moral complexity. The settings of Virgil's eclogues sometimes have features of his own homeland around Mantua, and in general act, like the landscapes of his *Georgics*, as a glorified image of external nature made productive by the hand of man, as well as a mirror of man's feelings and desires. In references to contemporaries and to himself, Virgil develops a more thoroughly allegorical pastoral than Theocritus ever attempts, but Virgil's Christian medieval successors carry allegory to crudely extravagant lengths, so that by the time of Mantuanus pastoral poetry is almost invariably concerned wholly with nonpastoral life in court, church, and city, and frequently discusses public issues in a quite un-Virgilian vein of satire.

This Christianized, elaborately allegorical version of Virgilian pastoral was imported into England by Sidney and Spenser, and transformed utterly. At its lowest, allegory could degenerate into the finicky correspondences and drab didacticism of Barclay or Googe, but at its highest it provided the poet with a never-fading symbol of the artist's imagination itself—Sannazaro's Arcadia, Spenser's Mount Acidale, Drayton's Muses' Elizium. The Elizabethans were clearly fascinated by the notion of poet-as-shepherd: "the sad shepherd" uttering his love-lament was undoubtedly the most favored personae among lyric poets generally, but, more importantly, the finest of Sidney's, Spenser's, and Drayton's allegorical pastoral writings—where the shepherd reflects upon his craft—are, in effect, visionary meditations upon the wonder and holiness of poetry. The most accomplished of all these poet-shepherds is surely Milton, who perfected Renaissance Christian allegorical pastoral in an elegy which is at once wholly derivative and intensely personal.

Spenser, Sidney, and Milton are typical Renaissance poets in their

belief that art completes and perfects imperfect nature (a belief
implicit in the highly wrought creations of Theocritus and Virgil).
Pope is the last great pastoral poet of their kind: he took pastoral
poetry as far as it was reasonably possible toward pure aesthetic patterning and the creation of lovely forms not bound to any particular
exterior or factual "reality." Spenser, Milton, and Pope, each in his
turn absorbed the literary pastoral tradition of his age and fixed it
in some single, monumental work of art; but in the course of a little
over a century between Spenser and Pope the tradition itself became
narrower and more detached from the chief moral and intellectual
concerns of man. In their pastorals, Spenser, Sidney, and Milton are
concerned intensely with serious, living moral and aesthetic ideals,
though the doctrinal issues raised by Spenser and Milton have perhaps a less enduring vitality: Pope's pastorals, lovely as they are, are
smaller than theirs in significance and scope. Even so, little Pope is a
giant in his time: for most of his contemporaries allegorical pastoral
had been simplified to a merely conventional bucolic masquerade,
where court rakes or university scholars pretended quite unseriously to
be shepherds. Writings by Rapin, Fontenelle, and their tiresome but
tireless English disciples betray the empty academism of theories of
pastoral current at the end of the seventeenth century. Earlier, in circumstances similar to those in which Virgil wrote his eclogues, Marvell broke away almost completely from the Spenserian–Miltonic line
in order to play with pastoral conventions in a witty, half-humorous
dialectic on nature and art. He developed a distinctive, highly individual "pastoral of the self," but his work had no progeny.
     Much English pastoral, from Spenser onward, was characterized
by patriotism and a love of the English countryside. Elizabethan
pastoral poets sought to moderate Golden Age fantasy by the use of
concrete rustic detail from English scenery and folklore, and to in-
vigorate their art by injections from rustic popular song and ballad.
Drayton, Browne, and Herrick, in their different ways, all held an
even balance between the Arcadia of pure art and the workaday
English countryside. The notion of an "English Arcadia" was latent
in Elizabethan pastoral, but in the earlier seventeenth century it was
clearly defined by a generation of nostalgic poets in the face of threats
from Puritanism and commercialized farming. Theocritean–Virgilian
pastoral feeling, reinforced by idyllic sentiments taken, somewhat out
of context, from Horace's *Odes* and Virgil's *Georgics*, flowed into

a great body of seventeenth- and eighteenth-century poetry on rural themes; so that the eclogue became only one, and not the most important, vehicle for "pastoral" ideas about the moral superiority of country life over court and city. The eighteenth century, by and large, simply opposed art to nature, and came at last to favor the latter. Inspired in part by misconceived notions about the simplicity and realism of Theocritus, poets sought to rediscover the roots of authentic pastoral in rural society. Gay's *The Shepherd's Week* is outstanding and exceptional in its saving wit, but the blend of idyll and observation which makes up most "naturalized" pastoral in this century tends inevitably to be sentimental. Insofar as this poetry has any informing ideas, these are patronizing humanitarian doctrines of natural goodness, natural genius, and sympathy. It is widely agreed that the rural poor demand a song, though not the kind of song sung by Crabbe, and, under the stimulus of primitivist aesthetic theories, genuine bucolic poets from Duck to Bloomfield were encouraged to sing this song themselves.

For two centuries, the course of events—the Civil War, the growth of London, enclosures, and industrialization— gave a tenuous validity to a kind of English rural Golden Age myth. This took the form of a vague memory of rural joy and innocence destroyed by Puritanism, commerce, industry, or some other hated feature of modern and urban existence. With varying degrees of plausibility, several generations of poets superimpose the pastoral myth upon the observed reality of rural life, see that it conforms to some of the facts of that life, and thereupon presume that it corresponds to all of the facts. The myth is plain to view in *Annalia Dubrensia*, it lies buried deep in Marvell, and it clearly shapes Goldsmith's Auburn and the threatened society of Lakeland peasants in Wordsworth's soberly primitivist verse and his letter to Fox. The myth gradually becomes more democratic, and about the beginning of the nineteenth century begins to operate in the world of fact, when the dream of a lost English rural Golden Age enters into working-class movements in the writings of Cobbett.

Wordsworth both embraced and transcended the whole eighteenth-century tradition of rural verse, much as Spenser did the whole Renaissance pastoral tradition. Spenser's pastoral world is a metaphor of spiritual, moral, and artistic integrity, in which social referents (found chiefly in the religious satire) are subsidiary; whereas Wordsworth claims to represent social realities in specific localities in late eighteenth-century England. In works as different as *The Prelude* and his Lake District *Guide*, he establishes pastoral in the contemporary social and political world, and in his letter to Charles James Fox about "Michael" he insists that the lessons of pastoral are to be applied in that world. When, in the letter, he calls the shepherd's little tract of land a "tablet" of feelings and a "fountain" of affection, he propounds a sociopolitical doctrine, but he also restates one of the old truths of pastoral poetry. As Colin Clout's landscape is a mirror of his feelings, so Michael's fields and unfinished sheepfold are the book which records his moral life: they are the mirror of his hopes and disappointments. The story of Michael is Wordsworth's artistic manifesto, the assertion of simplicity and truth against romantic fiction, and an affirmation of the powers and responsibilities of poetry which is as effective, in its completely different mode, as Colin's. Wordsworth's pastoral world, like Spenser's, is a metaphor of spiritual, moral, and artistic integrity. When Wordsworth addresses youthful poets who will be his "second self," we sense the continuity of a tradition—the continuity implied in Theocritus's seventh idyll as Lycidas presents his wild-olive staff to Simichidas. When nature is said to mourn Daphnis, Thyrsis speaks "with a voice / Obedient to the strong creative power / Of human passion." Contemplating Michael's unfinished sheepfold, Wordsworth expresses sympathies

> More tranquil, yet perhaps of kindred birth,
> That steal upon the meditative mind,
> And grow with thought.

Daphnis and Michael are worlds apart, but in their tragic, consoling histories, Theocritus and Wordsworth alike explore the herdsman's life as a way of feeling and knowing, and a means by which a poet may learn his art.

Notes and References

Chapter One

1. W. W. Tarn, *Hellenistic Civilization*, 3d ed., rev. (London: Arnold, 1952), p. 1.
2. Translations from Theocritus are from R. C. Trevelyan, *A Translation of the Idylls of Theocritus* (Cambridge: Cambridge University Press, 1947), introduction dated 1925. Trevelyan preserves the Greek forms of proper names; elsewhere in the present study the more familiar Latin forms generally are used.
3. See B. F. Dick, "Ancient Pastoral and the Pathetic Fallacy," *Comparative Literature* 20 (1968):27–44, where Theocritus's relatively simple use of the pathetic fallacy is contrasted with Virgil's more subtle use.
4. Idylls 1–7 (i.e., including 2 with its urban setting) have a certain unity of theme and form. Their interrelations are discussed in G. Lawall, *Theocritus' Coan Pastorals, A Poetry Book* (Cambridge, Mass., 1967).
5. The commentary in A. S. F. Gow, *Theocritus*, 2 vols. (Cambridge: Cambridge University Press, 1950), identifies most topographical references.
6. See Lawall, *Theocritus' Coan Pastorals*, pp. 102–8.
7. "Arcady" is merely a geographical term here; it does not yet possess the ideal, Golden Age associations that Virgil and, particularly, Sannazaro, were to attach to it.
8. Preface to *Lyrical Ballads* (1800).
9. A. S. F. Gow, *The Greek Bucolic Poets, Translated with Brief Notes* (Cambridge: Cambridge University Press, 1953), p. 147.
10. Daphnis, in the first idyll of Theocritus, is probably an Adonis-cult figure: see William Berg, *Early Virgil* (London: Athlone Press, 1974), pp. 12–22.
11. Gow, *Greek Bucolic Poets*, p. 153.

Chapter Two

1. For the argument that eclogue 9 is idyll 7 "in reverse," see Berg,

Early Virgil, pp. 138–42. Berg's book is a good account of the *Eclogues* as Virgil's exploration of the role of a poet.

2. Antony's expected child is the more likely candidate. See W. W. Tarn, "Alexander Helios and the Golden Age," *Journal of Roman Studies* 22 (1932):135–60.

3. All likely parallels and some others are indicated in T. F. Royds, *Virgil and Isaiah* (Oxford: B. H. Blackwell, 1918).

4. Virgil is one of the principal channels through which the Golden Age myth descends to modern literature: others are Ovid, *Metamorphoses*, bk. 1, ll. 89–150, and Boethius, *De Consolatione Philosophiae*, 2, 5. The myth or something comparable to it occurs in every culture, as a perpetual protest against the present human condition.

5. On the elaborate symmetrical structure of Virgil's *Eclogues* see Berg, *Early Virgil*, pp. 107–13.

6. Brooks Otis, *Virgil: a Study in Civilized Poetry* (Oxford: Clarendon Press, 1963), p. 136.

7. The symbolic function of landscape is examined in impressive detail in E. W. Leach, *Vergil's Eclogues: Landscapes of Experience* (Ithaca, 1974).

8. Theocritus makes topographical references to Arcadia in his idylls 2, line 48, and 7, line 107; but Virgil first makes the indissoluble identification of shepherd-poet with Arcadian. In eclogue 10, for instance, "Arcadians are the only folk who know how to sing."

9. For the argument that it is not in the *Eclogues* but in the *Georgics* that Virgil's most mature examination of *otium* is to be found, see P. J. Davis, "Vergil's Georgics and the Pastoral Ideal," *Ramus: Critical Studies in Greek and Roman Literature* 8 (1979):22–33.

10. *Eclogues of Virgil*, trans. C. Day Lewis (London: Jonathan Cape, 1963), p. 8.

11. G. Highet, *Poets in a Landscape* (London: Hamish Hamilton, 1957), p. 138.

12. *Collected Works of R. C. Trevelyan* (London: Longmans, 1939), 1:352.

13. *Minor Latin Poets*, trans. J. W. and A. M. Duff, Loeb Classical Library (London: Heinemann, 1934), pp. 220–21. This volume also contains the *Eclogues* of Nemesianus.

Chapter Three

1. W. L. Grant, *Neo-Latin Literature and the Pastoral* (Chapel Hill, 1965), p. 87. A more recent and more wide-ranging study by Helen Cooper, *Pastoral: Medieval into Renaissance* (Ipswich, 1977), makes broadly the same point.

2. Grant, *Neo-Latin Literature and the Pastoral*, p. 103.

3. Thus Phoebus in Milton's *Lycidas*, and Pan in his *Hymn on the Morning of Christ's Nativity*. In Spenser's *The Shepheardes Calender* Pan, true to his name, is at once the wood-god of ancient myth, Almighty God and Henry VIII.

4. See E. R. Curtius, *European Literature and the Latin Middle Ages*, trans. W. R. Trask (London: Routledge, 1953), p. 200, n. 31; and A. B. Giamatti, *The Earthly Paradise and the Renaissance Epic* (Princeton: Princeton University Press, 1966), pp. 11–93.

5. Grant, *Neo-Latin Literature and the Pastoral*, pp. 133–34.

6. IV, ii, 92–93. (New Arden edition).

7. Grant, *Neo-Latin Literature and the Pastoral*, index, *sub* Henry Anderson, John Barclay, George Buchanan, David Hume, Arthur Johnston, and John Leech.

8. W. W. Greg, *Pastoral Poetry and Pastoral Drama* (London, 1906), p. 29.

9. Jacopo Sannazaro, *Arcadia and Piscatorial Eclogues*, trans. Ralph Nash (Detroit: Wayne State University Press, 1966), pp. 29–30.

10. See E. Panofsky, *"Et in Arcadia ego:* On the Conception of Transience in Poussin and Watteau,"* in *Philosophy and History, Essays presented to Ernst Cassirer*, ed. R. Klibansky and H. J. Paton (Oxford: Clarendon Press, 1936), pp. 223–54.

11. *The Eclogues of Alexander Barclay from the original edition by John Cawood*, ed. Beatrice White, Early English Text Society (London: Oxford University Press, 1928).

12. *Eglogs, Epytaphes and Sonettes*, ed. Edward Arber, English Reprints, vol. 30 (London, 1871).

13. *The Eclogues of Mantuan, Translated by G. Turbervile*, ed. D. Bush (New York: Scholars' Facsimiles and Reprints, 1937). In his introduction Bush assesses the influence of Mantuan on English verse.

Chapter Four

1. Except for ecclesiastical satire, the principal themes of *The Shepheardes Calender* can be traced to Theocritus and Virgil, but Spenser's immediate models were mostly Renaissance. See M. Y. Hughes, *Virgil and Spenser* (Berkeley: University of California Press, 1929). Spenser's handling of his sources, particularly his adaptations from Mantuan and Marot as a result of his superior critical understanding of Virgil, is discussed in Nancy Jo Hoffman, *Spenser's Pastorals* (Baltimore: Johns Hopkins University Press, 1977), pp. 9–41.

2. The meters used in *The Shepheardes Calender* are listed in W. L. Renwick, *Edmund Spenser, an Essay on Renaissance Poetry* (London:

Arnold, 1925), p. 189. See also John Thompson, *The Founding of English Metre* (London: Routledge, 1961).

3. On the question of political and ecclesiastical allegory in *The Shepheardes Calender* see Paul E. McLane, *Spenser's Shepheards Calender: a Study in Elizabethan Allegory* (Notre Dame: University of Notre Dame Press, 1961). McLane discusses in particular detail Spenser's allegorical treatment of two burning and dangerous topical issues: the unpopular negotiations for the Queen's marriage with the Duke of Alençon, and the systematic plundering of the church by corrupt prelates and laypatrons. For a broader treatment of allegory see Isabel G. MacCaffrey, "Allegory and Pastoral in *The Shepheardes Calender*," *English Literary History* 36 (1969):88–109.

4. The first view is termed "Mantuanesque" and the second "Arcadian" in a suggestive analysis by Patrick Cullen, *Spenser, Marvell and Renaissance Pastoral* (Cambridge, Mass., 1970), pp. 29–76.

5. Quotations from *The Shepheardes Calender* are from the variorum edition of *The Works of Edmund Spenser*; Vol. 1, *The Minor Poems*, ed. C. G. Osgood et al. (Baltimore: Johns Hopkins Press, 1943).

6. The poem is discussed as an "inimitable poetic description of puberty" by Leo Spitzer, "Spenser, *Shepheardes Calender, March*," *Studies in Philology* 47 (1950):494–505.

7. "Discourse on Pastoral Poetry," in *Poems of Alexander Pope*, ed. John Butt (London: Methuen, 1963), p. 122.

8. Spenser leaves his readers in doubt as to whether Calidore's pastoral retirement is a reprehensible truancy from his chivalric quest, or the essential proving ground for his courtesy (which must work in humble society as well as in courts). See J. C. Maxwell, "The Truancy of Calidore," in *That Soueraine Light, Essays in Honor of Edmund Spenser*, ed. W. R. Mueller and D. C. Allen (Baltimore: Johns Hopkins Press, 1952), pp. 63–69. Donald Chesney, in *Spenser's Image of Nature: Wild Man and Shepherd in "The Faerie Queene"* (New Haven: Yale University Press, 1966), suggests that pastoralism is implicit throughout all six books of the poem; so that the Pastorella episode, in which the narrator of *The Faerie Queene*, Colin Clout, emerges, should be seen not as an interlude but as the climax of the whole work.

9. That is, the "Old Arcadia," in *The Countess of Pembroke's Arcadia*, ed. Jean Robertson (Oxford: Clarendon Press, 1973).

10. Quotations from Sidney's verse are from *The Countess of Pembroke's Arcadia*, ed. Jean Robertson.

11. Jean Robertson, "Sir Philip Sidney and his Poetry," *Elizabethan Poetry*, ed. J. R. Brown and B. Harris (London: Edward Arnold, 1960), p. 125.

12. *Seven Types of Ambiguity* (London: Chatto and Windus, 1930), p. 48. There is an excellent detailed analysis of Sidney's double sestina in David Kalstone, *Sidney's Poetry* (Cambridge: Harvard University Press, 1965), pp. 71–85.

13. Barley-break is defined in *N.E.D.* as follows: "An old country game... played by six persons (three of each sex) in couples; one couple being left in the middle den termed 'hell,' had without breaking hands to catch the others who were allowed to separate or 'break' when hard pressed, and thus change partners, but had when caught to take their turn as catchers." The first citation in *N.E.D.* is from Machyn's *Diary* (1557) and uses the game as an image of adultery. The game makes frequent appearances in Elizabethan writing, and particularly in pastoral. In John Lyly's *Midas* (1591), V, iii, 12, "*Apollo* is tuning his pipes, or at barly-breake with *Daphne*." In Drayton's *Endimon and Phoebe* and the First and Third "Nimphalls" of *The Muses Elizium* it is played variously by satyrs, nymphs and fairies. It is referred to in Browne's *Britannia's Pastorals*, book 1 (1613), song 3, and in Wither's *Fidelia* (1615), where it is an image of lovers' misunderstandings. It was sometimes associated with wantonness. Thus the Hertfordshire fairies in Drayton's *Poly-Olbion*, part 2 (1612), song 21, "Oft runne at Barley-breake upon the eares of Corne; / And catching drops of dew in their lascivious chases..." (ll. 98–99). Herrick characteristically approves:

> We two are last in Hell: what may we feare
> To be tormented, or kept pris'ners here?
> Alas! if kissing be of plagues the worst,
> We'll wish, in Hell we had been Last and First.
> ("Barly-Break: or, Last in Hell")

But this Hell becomes less innocent in the Jacobean dramatists: in, for example, Dekker and Massinger's *The Virgin Martyr* (1620) V, i, 101, or in Dekker's *Match me in London* (1623), IV, vi, 6, and Middleton and Rowley's *The Changeling* (1622), III, iii, 165, and V, iii, 163, where barley break is an image of adulterous relationships. A pastoral narrative poem about seduction and suicide under the title *Barley-Breake, or a warning for wantons,* by W. N. is summarized by Douglas Bush in *Mythology and the Renaissance Tradition*, pp. 327–28. Sir John Suckling's use of the game as a vehicle for moral allegory perhaps approaches closest to Sidney:

> Love, Reason, Hate did once bespeak
> Three mates to play at Barley-break.

Love Folly took, and Reason Fancy;
And Hate consorts with Pride; so dance they....

Their game continues through various combinations of couples, but every round ends with Love and Folly together in Hell.

14. Walter R. Davis, "A Map of Arcadia," in *Sidney's Arcadia*, by Walter R. Davis and Richard A. Lanham (New Haven: Yale University Press, 1965), p. 94.

15. George Puttenham, *The Art of English Poesie*, ed. G. D. Willcock and A. Walker (Cambridge: Cambridge University Press, 1936), p. 38.

Chapter Five

1. *The Works of Michael Drayton*, ed. J. W. Hebel, 5 vols. (Oxford: Basil Blackwell, 1961), 2:517–18.

2. *Some Longer Elizabethan Poems*, intro. A. H. Bullen, in *An English Garner* (1903; reprint ed., New York: Cooper Square, 1964), p. 145.

3. Quotations from Barnfield are taken from *Some Longer Elizabethan Poems*, intro. Bullen.

4. Quotations from Drayton are taken from *The Works*, ed. Hebel.

5. This song had been published, with slight variations, in *England's Helicon* (1600).

6. See *The Works*, ed. Hebel, 5:206–9, and authorities cited there. Hebel links Drayton's poem with Browne's *The Shepheards Pipe* (1614), Wither's *The Shepheard's Hunting*, and those satires which earned Wither royal displeasure and landed him in prison.

7. The identification of Felicia with England is argued in R. F. Hardin, *Michael Drayton and the passing of Elizabethan England* (Lawrence: University of Kansas Press, 1973), pp. 127–31. Hardin treats Drayton as essentially a poet of nostalgic patriotism.

8. Quotations from Browne are taken from *The Works*, ed. G. Goodwin, 2 vols. (London: Routledge, 1894).

Chapter Six

1. *England's Helicon*, ed. Hugh Macdonald (London: Routledge, 1950). Quotations are from this edition.

2. A. K. Moore, *The Secular Lyric in Middle English* (Lexington: University of Kentucky Press, 1951), p. 55, argues that only three Middle English lyrics are, strictly speaking, "pastourelles," though elements of that form may be found in many other lyrics and ballads. On

the share of the pastourelle element in the development of Elizabethan pastoral, see Cooper, *Pastoral, Medieval into Renaissance,* 1977).

3. F. J. Child, *The English and Scottish Popular Ballads* (Boston: Houghton Mifflin, 1884–98), no. 112.

4. C. R. Baskerville, *The Elizabethan Jig* (Chicago: Chicago University Press, 1929), chap. 1.

5. E. K. Chambers and F. Sidgwick, *Early English Lyrics* (London: Sidgwick and Jackson, 1907), nos. 28–29.

6. *The Shirburn Ballads, 1585–1616,* ed. Andrew Clark (Oxford: Clarendon Press, 1907), pp. 220–22.

7. Reprinted in V. de S. Pinto and A. E. Rodway, *The Common Muse* (London: Chatto and Windus, 1957), pp. 223–25; and in J. S. Farmer, *Merry songs and Ballads* (London: privately printed, 1895–97), 2:30–33.

8. Many imitations are listed in R. S. Forsythe, "*The Passionate Shepherd* and English Poetry," *PMLA* 40 (1925):692–742.

9. *Poems by Nicholas Breton,* ed. Jean Robertson (Liverpool: Liverpool University Press, 1952), p. lxxxvii. Robertson notes "There were of course many other poems written in imitation of Marlowe's invitation, but I do not recall any other example of the refrain turned to devotional purposes."

10. Pinto and Rodway, *The Common Muse,* p. 228.

11. *Complete Works in Verse and Prose of Samuel Daniel,* ed. A. B. Grosart (Aylesbury: For private circulation, 1885–96), 1:261.

Chapter Seven

1. E. H. Fellowes, *English Madrigal Verse, 1588–1632,* rev. F. W. Sternfield and D. Greer (Oxford: Clarendon Press, 1967), pp. 158–66.

2. Reprinted in facsimile by the Scolar Press (Menston, Yorkshire, 1973). See also C. Whitfield, *Robert Dover and the Cotswold Games* (London: Henry Sotheran, 1962).

3. John Brand, *Observations on Popular Antiquities,* rev. H. Ellis (London: Knight's Miscellanies, 1841), 1:136.

4. *Poems by Nicholas Breton,* ed. Jean Robertson (Liverpool: Liverpool University Press, 1952).

5. See R. H. Tawney, *The Agrarian Problem in the Sixteenth Century* (London: Longmans, 1912), and M. W. Beresford, *The Lost Villages of England* (London: Lutterworth Press, 1954).

6. *Collected Poems of Joseph Hall,* ed. A. Davenport (Liverpool: Liverpool University Press, 1949); "wales" may mean "choices" (*N.E.D.,* wale, sb. ^{2}), though Davenport in his note on this passage

ingeniously suggests that it may refer to America, in allusion to the re-discovery of that continent by Madoc ap Owen Gwynedd, ca. 1170.

7. *Works*, ed. P. Hall (Oxford: Talboys, 1837–9), 5:195.

8. "Six Ballads," ed. James Goodwin, in *Early English Poetry*, Percy Society, vol. 13 (1844).

9. W. Chappell, *Popular Music of the Olden Time* (London: Cramer, Beale, and Chappell, 1959), 2:464.

10. The portion of this line running from Jonson to Pope is discussed in G. R. Hibbard, "The Country House Poem of the Seventeenth Century," *Journal of the Warburg and Courtauld Institutes* 19 (1956):159–74; see also C. Molesworth, "Property and Virtue," *Genre* 1 (1968): 141–57; and James Turner, *The Politics of Landscape: Rural Scenery and Society in English Poetry 1630–1660* (Oxford: Clarendon Press, 1979). For a demonstration that idealization in the country-house poems is a "cheat," see Raymond Williams, *The Country and the City* (London: Chatto and Windus, 1973), pp. 26–34.

11. *Poems of Thomas Carew*, ed. R. Dunlap (Oxford: Clarendon Press, 1949), p. 49.

12. *Poems of Richard Lovelace*, ed. C. H. Wilkinson (Oxford: Clarendon Press, 1930), p. 146.

13. Quotations from Herrick are from the *Poetical Works*, ed. L. C. Martin (Oxford: Clarendon Press, 1956).

14. Paul Hentzner, traveling near Windsor in 1598, observed a Hock Cart: "As we were returning to our inn we happened to meet some country people celebrating their Harvest Home; their last load of corn they crown with flowers, having besides an image richly dressed, by which perhaps they would signify Ceres: this they keep moving about, while men and women, men and maid-servants, riding through the streets in the cart, shout as loud as they can till they arrive at the barn" (Brand, *Observations on Popular Antiquities*, 2:14).

15. See the excellent criticism of this poem in Cleanth Brooks, *The Well Wrought Urn* (London: Denis Dobson, 1949), pp. 62–73.

16. "On the Inestimable Content he enjoys in the Muses." This, and other quotations from Randolph, are taken from *Poems*, ed. G. Thorn-Drury (London: Haslewood Books, 1929).

Chapter Eight

1. H. M. Richmond, "Rural Lyricism: A Renaissance Mutation of the Pastoral," *Comparative Literature* 16 (1964):193–210.

2. Quotations from Milton and translations (by Walter Skeat) of the Latin Poems are from *Milton, Complete Poetry and Selected Prose*, ed. E. H. Visiak (London: Nonesuch Press, 1948).

3. There is a comprehensive collection of *Lycidas* criticism in *A Variorum Commentary on the Poems of John Milton*, vol. 2, ed. A. S. P. Woodhouse and Douglas Bush (London: Routledge, 1972), pt. 2; and a useful selection in *Milton's Lycidas, the Tradition and the Poem*, ed. C. A. Patrides (New York: Holt, Rinehart and Winston, 1961).

4. Maynard Mack, *Milton* (Englewood Cliffs, N.J.: Prentice-Hall, 1950), p. 10.

5. Ibid.

6. Some bizarre examples of this tendency in Milton may be found in his Latin elegy on the death of the bishop of Winchester, which utilizes tags from the erotic verse of Ovid and Tibullus.

7. For evidence that it is not beyond all conjecture, see *A Variorum Commentary on the Poems of John Milton*, vol. 2 (1972), pt. 2, pp. 686–706.

8. See John R. Knott, Jr., *Milton's Pastoral Vision: an Approach to Paradise Lost* (Chicago: University of Chicago Press, 1971).

9. Quotations from Marvell are from *The Poems and Letters of Andrew Marvell*, ed. H. M. Margoliouth, 3d ed. (Oxford: Clarendon Press, 1971), vol. 1, revised by Pierre Legouis with the collaboration of E. E. Duncan-Jones.

10. On "The Garden" as "pastoral of the self" see Renato Poggioli, *The Oaten Flute* (Cambridge, Mass, 1975), pp. 174–80.

11. *Poems and Letters of Andrew Marvell*, ed. H. M. Margoliouth, 3d ed. (1971), 1:266.

12. Donald M. Friedman, *Marvell's Pastoral Art* (London: Routledge, 1970), p. 120. This work is the fullest and best-balanced discussion of pastoral in Marvell's poetry.

13. For a detailed exposition see D. C. Allen, *Image and Meaning*, rev. ed. (Baltimore: Johns Hopkins Press, 1968), pp. 201–12.

Chapter Nine

1. "Local poetry" is Johnson's term for the new genre initiated by *Cooper's Hill*. Most of such poetry is rural in subject and idyllic in tone; see R. A. Aubin, *Topographical Poetry in XVIII-Century England* (New York: Modern Language Association of America, 1936).

2. Reprinted in Pinto and Rodway, *The Common Muse*, pp. 229–33.

3. *The English Poets*, ed. Alexander Chalmers (1810), 8:345.

4. *Minor Poets of the Caroline Period*, ed. G. Saintsbury (Oxford: Clarendon Press, 1905), vol. 3.

5. The origins of this debate and its progress through eighteenth-century English criticism are documented in J. E. Congleton, *Theories of Pastoral Poetry in England, 1684–1798* (Gainesville, 1952).

6. Quotations from Pope are from the Twickenham Edition of the *Poems*, vol. 1, ed. E. Audra and A. Williams (London: Methuen, 1961).

7. Geoffrey Tillotson, *On the Poetry of Pope*, 2d ed. (Oxford: Clarendon Press, 1950), p. 127. Tillotson also discusses in greater detail the diction of line 19: see his *Augustan Poetic Diction* (London: Athlone Press, 1964), pp. 32–33.

8. Jeffry B. Spencer, *Heroic Nature: Ideal Landscape in English Poetry from Marvell to Thomson* (Evanston: Northwestern University Press, 1973), p. 201.

9. Oliver Goldsmith, *The Art of Poetry on a New Plan* (London, 1762), 1:84.

10. The authoritative critical survey of retirement verse to 1760 is M. S. Røstvig, *The Happy Man*, vol. 2 (Oslo, 1958).

11. There is a useful census, with some discussion, of the nonpastoral eclogue in R. F. Jones, "Eclogue Types in English Poetry of the Eighteenth Century," *JEGP* 24 (1925).

Chapter Ten

1. Quotations are from *John Gay: Poetry and Prose*, ed. V. A. Dearing, with the assistance of C. E. Beckwith (Oxford: Clarendon Press, 1974). For criticism of *Rural Sports* and *The Shepherd's Week*, see A. Forsgren, *John Gay, Poet of a Lower Order* (Stockholm: Natur och Kultur, 1964).

2. Quotations are from *The Works of Allan Ramsay*, ed. B. Martin, J. W. Oliver, A. M. Kinghorn, and A. Law, 6 vols. (Edinburgh: William Blackwood, 1945–74).

3. Quotations are from *The Tea-Table Miscellany*, 2 vols. (Edinburgh: Alex. Donaldson, 1775).

4. Keith Stewart, "The Ballad and the *Genres* in the Eighteenth Century," *ELH* 24 (1957):125.

5. Joseph Warton, *An Essay on Pope* (1756), p. 3; *The Works of Virgil* (1753), II, ii, 68.

6. Quotation is from *The Seasons and the Castle of Indolence*, ed. James Sambrook (Oxford: Clarendon Press, 1972). On the georgic in general, and *The Seasons* in particular, see John Chalker, *The English Georgic* (Baltimore: Johns Hopkins Press, 1969).

7. Some are discussed in Robert Southey, introductory essay to *Attempts in Verse by John Jones* (London, 1831); C. B. Tinker, *Nature's Simple Plan* (Princeton: Princeton University Press, 1922); and Rayner Unwin, *The Rural Muse* (London: Allen and Unwin, 1954.)

8. A case for the precise location of Goldsmith's deserted village is argued in Mavis Batey, "Nuneham Courtenay: an Oxfordshire 18th Cen-

tury Deserted Village," *Oxoniensia* 33 (1968):108–24, and 43 (1978): 258.

9. Goldsmith quotations are from the *Collected Works*, ed. A. Friedman (Oxford: Clarendon Press, 1966), vols. 3–4.

10. *Correspondence of Edmund Burke*, ed. J. A. Woods (Cambridge: Cambridge University Press, 1963), 4:234.

11. See A. J. Sambrook, "The English Lord and the Happy Husbandman," *Studies in Voltaire and the Eighteenth Century* 57 (1967):1357–75; and "Some Heirs of Goldsmith: Poets of the Poor in the late Eighteenth Century," *Studies in Burke and his Time* 11 (1969):1348–61.

12. Cowper quotations are from the *Poetical Works*, ed. H. S. Milford, 4th ed., corr. N. Russell (London: Oxford University Press, 1967).

13. Crabbe quotations are from the *Poems*, ed. A. W. Ward (Cambridge: Cambridge University Press, 1905), vol. 1.

Chapter Eleven

1. Quotations are from *William Wordsworth: Poems*, ed. John O. Hayden, 2 vols. (Harmondsworth: Penguin Books, 1977).

2. These poems are discussed in S. M. Parrish, "The Ballad as Pastoral," *The Art of the Lyrical Ballads* (Cambridge: Harvard University Press, 1973), pp. 149–87.

3. Quotations are from *William Wordsworth: The Prelude, a Parallel Text*, ed. J. C. Maxwell (Harmondsworth: Penguin Books, 1971).

4. Harold E. Toliver, *Pastoral Forms and Attitudes* (Berkeley, 1971), p. 258.

5. F. W. Bateson, *Wordsworth, a Re-interpretation*, 2d ed. (London: Longmans, 1956), p. 200.

6. Ibid. See also Helen Darbishire, *The Poet Wordsworth* (Oxford: Clarendon Press, 1950), pp. 35–53.

Selected Bibliography

Alpers, Paul. "The Eclogue Tradition and the Nature of Pastoral." *College English* 34 (1972):352–71. Compares conventions and poetic modes in Virgil's *Eclogues*, *The Shepheardes Calender*, and *Lycidas*.

———. *The Singer of the Eclogues: a Study of Virgilian Pastoral, with a new translation of the Eclogues*. Berkeley: University of California Press, 1979. This important study, which was published too late to be taken into account in the revision of my book, explores the intricate relationship in the *Eclogues* between representation of a community of shepherds and self-representation of the poet.

Arthos, John. *The Language of Natural Description in Eighteenth-Century Poetry*. Ann Arbor: University of Michigan Press, 1949. Lexicon of words and phrases taken by seventeenth- and eighteenth-century poets from classical poets: citations from Virgil are particularly interesting for the student of pastoral.

Barrell, John, and Bull, John. *The Penguin Book of English Pastoral Verse*. London: Allen Lane, 1974. Very substantial anthology, from sixteenth to twentieth century.

Bragg, Marion K. *The Formal Eclogue in Eighteenth-Century England*. Orono: Maine University Press, 1926. Many inaccuracies of names and dates, but remains the fullest survey of its subject.

Bush, Douglas. *Mythology and the Renaissance Tradition in English Poetry*. Minneapolis: University of Minnesota Press, 1932.

———. *Mythology and the Romantic Tradition in English Poetry*. Minneapolis: University of Minnesota Press, 1937. Two comprehensive works which describe the uses of classical mythology in English nondramatic poetry and contain much material on the pastoral.

Carrara, Enrico. *La Poesia Pastorale*. Milan: Storia dei Generi Letterari Italiani, 1909. A full history of Latin and vernacular Italian-Renaissance pastoral.

Chambers, E. K. *English Pastorals*. London: Blackie, 1905. An anthology, from late fifteenth to early eighteenth century, but with very few pieces later than Marvell. The lively introduction, a pioneer study which retains its value, was reprinted in *Sir Thomas Wyatt and some collected studies* (London, 1933).

Cody, Richard. *The Landscape of the Mind*. Oxford: Clarendon Press, 1969. Mostly on the drama; but the introduction links Renaissance pastoralism with the aesthetic Platonic tradition and Orphism.

Congleton, J. E. *Theories of Pastoral Poetry in England, 1684–1798*. Gainesville: University of Florida Press, 1952. Studies critical writings only, with virtually no reference to pastorals themselves: comprehensive in its field, it has an invaluable bibliography.

Cooper, Helen. *Pastoral: Mediaeval into Renaissance*. Ipswich, Mass.: D. S. Brewer, Totowa, N.J.: Rowman and Littlefield, 1977. Well-documented account of pastoral literature in the Middle Ages, and its contribution to Renaissance pastoral.

Cullen, Patrick. *Spenser, Marvell, and Renaissance Pastoral*. Cambridge: Harvard University Press, 1970. Demonstration of the malleability, complexity, and protean variety of pastoral, by means of comparative studies of Spenser and Marvell.

Empson, William. *Some Versions of Pastoral*. London: Chatto and Windus, 1935. Defines pastoral in a broad sense as "putting the complex into the simple." The book consists mainly of highly stimulating analyses of literary techniques and social implications of "pastoral" thus defined in the work of Shakespeare, Milton, Marvell, Gay, Lewis Carroll, and others.

Gerhardt, Mia I. *La Pastorale*. Assen: Van Gorcum, 1950. Substantial study of medieval pastourelle and Renaissance pastoral in Italy, Spain, and France, including drama and prose.

Grant, W. L. *Neo-Latin Literature and the Pastoral*. Chapel Hill: University of North Carolina Press, 1965. Very detailed: summarizes and quotes, in translation, from hundreds of neo-Latin pastorals, mostly of the fifteenth to seventeenth centuries.

Greg, Walter W. *Pastoral Poetry and Pastoral Drama*. London: A. H. Bullen, 1906. Mostly on drama before 1640, but a pioneer and still indispensable study of the origins of English pastoral generally.

Grundy, Joan. *The Spenserian Poets, a Study in Elizabethan and Jacobean Poetry*. London: Edward Arnold, 1969. Shows that, as pastoral poets, Drayton, Browne, Wither, and Giles and Phineas Fletcher were deeply conservative: "they looked back to the past with a conscious and aggressive nostalgia."

Hall, Henry M. *Idylls of Fishermen*. New York: Columbia University Press, 1912. History of piscatory eclogue from Theocritus to the eighteenth century, with special attention to English examples.

Harrison, T. P. *The Pastoral Elegy, an Anthology*. Austin: University of

Texas Press, 1939. Reprints greatest pastoral elegies, with translations of classical and European ones, and useful apparatus: particularly valuable record of parallel passages, relating each elegy to others in a clear and coherent tradition.

Heath-Stubbs, John. *The Pastoral.* London: Oxford University Press, 1969. Inaccurate dates and attributions, but a handy, brief historical sketch of English pastoral, including classical origins.

Highet, Gilbert. *The Classical Tradition.* Oxford: Clarendon Press, 1951. Historical account of Greek and Roman influences on Western literature: many references to pastoral.

Jones, R. F. "Eclogue Types in English Poetry of the Eighteenth Century." *JEGP* 24 (1925):33–60. Argues that in the eighteenth century the term "eclogue" signified a small static drama, rather than pastoral subject matter.

Jones, William P. *The Pastourelle.* Cambridge: Harvard University Press, 1931. Distinguishes courtly and popular elements in the medieval French pastourelle.

Kermode, Frank. *English Pastoral Poetry from the beginnings to Marvell.* London: Harrap, 1952. An anthology: the introduction is probably the best piece of criticism on English pastoral poetry.

Lawall, Gilbert. *Theocritus' Coan Pastorals, A Poetry Book.* Cambridge: Harvard University Press, 1967. A study of Theocritus's idylls 1–7 as a unity constituting a deliberate and fully elaborated pastoral vision of life, and the seed from which the European pastoral tradition grew.

Leach, Eleanor Winsor. *Virgil's* Eclogues: *Landscapes of Experience.* Ithaca: Cornell University Press, 1974. An exploration of the thematic patterns of individual eclogues, relating them to the unity and design of the collection as a whole, and paying particular attention to Roman ideas and habits of thought.

Lerner, Laurence. *The Uses of Nostalgia: Studies in Pastoral Poetry.* London: Chatto and Windus, 1972. On the literary forms which embody our idealization of the past.

Lindenberger, Herbert. "The Idyllic Moment: on Pastoral and Romanticism." *College English* 34 (1972):335–51. Argues that pastoral manifests itself in islandlike, intense moments: includes interesting comparisons between Virgil and Wordsworth.

McCoy, D. S. *Tradition and Convention, a Study of Periphrasis in English Pastoral Poetry from 1557 to 1715.* The Hague: Mouton, 1965. Shows how "abuses of diction" crept into pastoral, causing "abuses of meaning."

Marinelli, Peter V. *Pastoral*. London: Methuen, 1971. A long essay on certain pastoral themes, mostly in English literature: the Golden Age, Arcadia, courtly invasions of pastoral settings, and the retreat into childhood.

Nitchie, Elizabeth. *Vergil and the English Poets*. New York: Columbia University Press, 1919. On English imitations of Virgil, including his *Eclogues*.

Poggioli, Renato. *The Oaten Flute: Essays on Pastoral Poetry and the Pastoral Ideal*. Cambridge: Harvard University Press, 1975. A study of the psychology of pastoral, as the literary form which expresses in its essence the wish-fulfilling function of art: the detailed critical discussion is mostly of post-Renaissance European literature.

Putnam, Michael C. J. *Virgil's Pastoral Art: Studies in the* Eclogues. Princeton: Princeton University Press, 1970. A very close and detailed structural analysis of each eclogue.

Richmond, H. M. "Rural Lyricism: a Renaissance Mutation of the Pastoral." *Comparative Literature* 16 (1964):193–210. Traces the process by which, in the sixteenth and seventeenth centuries, a modern genre of landscape poetry separated from conventional pastoral.

Røstvig, Maren-Sofie. *The Happy Man*. 2 vols. Vol. 1, rev. Oslo: Oslo University Press, 1958–62. Thorough, fully documented history of the "Happy-Man" Horatian-Virgilian motif in English literature, 1600–1760, a tradition which intermingles with formal pastoral.

Rosenmayer, Thomas G. *The Green Cabinet: Theocritus and the European Pastoral Lyric*. Berkeley: University of California Press, 1969. A wide-ranging, systematic study of the Theocritean tradition.

Smith, Hallett. *Elizabethan Poetry*. Cambridge: Harvard University Press, 1952. Chapter 1, "Pastoral Poetry, the Vitality and Versatility of a Convention," is a most important critical survey.

Snell, Bruno. "Arcadia, the discovery of a Spiritual Landscape." In *The Discovery of the Mind, the Greek Origins of European Thought*. Translated by T. G. Rosenmayer. Oxford: Blackwell, 1953. In the *Eclogues* Virgil shows himself as the first modern poet, "of fancies and dreams," whose feelings are more profound than other men's.

Tayler, Edward William. *Nature and Art in Renaissance Literature*. New York: Columbia University Press, 1964. Examines ways in which pastoralists deal overtly with the philosophical problem of Nature versus Art.

Tinker, C. B. *Nature's Simple Plan*. Princeton: Princeton University Press, 1922. Lively account of eighteenth-century primitivism and cult of the peasant-poet.

Toliver, Harold E. *Pastoral Forms and Attitudes*. Berkeley: University
of California Press, 1971. A broad survey from the sixteenth to the
twentieth century, with always illuminating discussions of particular texts: concentrates on themes and attitudes rather than strictly on
forms.

Wormell, D. E. W. "The Originality of the Eclogues." In *Virgil*. Edited
by D. R. Dudley. London: Routledge, 1969. Catches the distinctive
quality of the *Eclogues*.

Index

Addison, Joseph, 98, 103, 114
Adonis, 5, 10, 12, 13, 16, 42, 48–49, 81, 134
Aeneas Sylvius, 33
Anderson, Henry, 141n7
Anderson, Robert, 111
Annalia Dubrensia, 68–69, 71, 137
Antony, 21
Aphrodite, 3, 12, 48–49
Apollo, 12, 20, 28, 37, 55, 83–84, 86–87
Apollonius Rhodius, 2, 7, 11
Arcadia, 5, 13, 17–18, 23, 26, *30–33,* *43–47,* 50, 51, 53, 64, 71, 80, 97, 110, 116, 118, 130, 135–36
Aristotle, 2
Arnold, Matthew, 132
Artemidorus, 14
Augustine, St., 21

ballads, *59–61,* 72, 73, 111
Barclay, Alexander, 30, *33–34,* 35, 39, 74, 135
Barclay, John, 141n7
barley-break, 47, 52, 69, *143–44*n13
Barnes, William, 132
Barnfield, Richard, *49–51,* 62
Bateson, F. W., 132
Bion, *12–13,* 14, 37, 42, 49, 82–83, 99
Biacklock, Thomas, 103
Blake, William, 132
Bloomfield, Robert, *122–23,* 137

Boccaccio, *28–29,* 30
Bradshaw, Thomas, 49
Brerewood, Thomas, 103
Breton, Nicholas, 61, *63–65,* 70–71
Browne, Moses, 104
Browne, William, 51, *56–58,* 59, 71, 80, 98, 136
Buchanan, George, 141n7
Burke, Edmund, 116, 120
Burns, Robert, 122
Byron, John, 103

Calpurnius Siculus, 26
Carew, Thomas, 74–75
Carey, Lucius, Lord Falkland, 74
Caroline, Queen, 114
Cervantes, 33
Charles I, 59, 68–69, 74–75, 92
Chaucer, Geoffrey, 37, 42, 52
Chettle, Henry, 51
Churchill, Charles, 104
Cicero, 98
Clare, John, 132
Clark, Ewan, 111
Claude, 116
Clough, A. H., 132
Cobbett, William, 137
Coleridge, S. T., 11, 131
Colin Clout, *36–43,* 44, 47, 51–52, 66, 138
Collins, William, 105, 106
Constable, Henry, 63
Congreve, William, 99, 131

155

158

ENGLISH PASTORAL POETRY

Milton, John, 30–31, 79–86, 95, 97, 129, 135–36
Montagu, Lady Mary Wortley, 104
Montaigne, 98
Montemayor, 33, 43
More, Sir Thomas, 72–73
Morley, Thomas, 67
Moschus, 12, 14, 49, 81, 99
Moss, Thomas, 115
Muses, 7, 9, 13, 37, 55, 70–71, 82, 134

Nemesianus, 26
Nero, 26
Norris, John, 31

Octavian, 19–22, 49
Orpheus, 81, 83
Otis, Brooks, 23
Ovid, 9, 45, 52, 56, 65, 86

Pales, 28, 68
Pan, 3, 12, 23, 28, 31, 38, 53, 58, 69, 71, 73, 80, 85–87
Paradise, 29, 39, 85–87, 91, 113, 129, 130, 132
Pasquil's Palinodia, 70
Passionate Pilgrim, 62, 64
pastourelle, 60–61, 96, 144–45n2
Pearl, 28
Peele, George, 51
Pembroke, Countess of, 42
Peter, St., 83–84
Petrarch, 27–28, 35, 81
Philips, Ambrose, 98–99, 107–108, 110, 116
Philips, John, 107
Philomela, 20, 62, 95
Phoebus, see Apollo
Phoenix Nest, 59
Pills to Purge Melancholy, 96, 103
Pius II, 33

Plato, 41, 47, 53, 85
Playford, Henry and John, 96
Pollio, 15, 17, 21, 104–105
Polyphemus, 2, 6–9, 13, 15, 17, 49, 62, 89, 93, 95, 134
Pope, Alexander, 22, 41, 72, 97, 99–103, 104–107, 110, 116, 123, 136
Pope, Walter, 96
Porter, Endymion, 75, 77
Poussin, 32–33
Prynne, William, 68
Puttenham, George, 47

Raleigh, Sir Walter, 42, 64, 95
Ramsay, Allen, 103, 110, 111–12, 119
Randolph, Thomas, 68, 77–78
Rapin, 97–99, 136
Ravenscroft, Thomas, 60, 65
Relph, Josiah, 110–11
Reynolds, Sir Joshua, 118
Richmond, H. M., 79
Roberts, W. H., 115
Robinson, John, 118
Rochester, Earl of, 97
Rogers, Samuel, 102
Ronsard, 37, 42
Rowe, Nicholas, 103
Rowland of the Rock, 51–53

Sackville, Charles, Earl of Dorset, 96
Sannazaro, 30–33, 43–44, 46, 51, 53, 56, 104, 135
Saturn, 20–22, 74
Scott, John, 118–19, 121
Scott, Sir Walter, 122
Sedley, Sir Charles, 97
Servius, 27
Shaftesbury, Earl of, 98
Shakespeare, William, 30, 50–52, 61, 130